Worshiping God, God's Way

Worshiping God, God's Way

A Biblical Perspective of the Origin of Worship

STEVEN E. URSPRINGER

WIPF & STOCK · Eugene, Oregon

WORSHIPING GOD, GOD'S WAY
A Biblical Perspective of the Origin of Worship

Copyright © 2021 Steven E. Urspringer. All rights reserved. Except for brief quotations in critical publications or reviews, no part of this book may be reproduced in any manner without prior written permission from the publisher. Write: Permissions, Wipf and Stock Publishers, 199 W. 8th Ave., Suite 3, Eugene, OR 97401.

Wipf & Stock
An Imprint of Wipf and Stock Publishers
199 W. 8th Ave., Suite 3
Eugene, OR 97401

www.wipfandstock.com

PAPERBACK ISBN: 978-1-7252-6874-6
HARDCOVER ISBN: 978-1-7252-6873-9
EBOOK ISBN: 978-1-7252-6872-2

November 8, 2021 10:16 AM

All Bible quotations, unless otherwise designated are from the ISV, NLT, NLT, NIV, NASB, or KJV.

Used by permission. Hebrew and Greek words are from Strong's and Vine's concordances.

For more information, contact worshipinggodgodsway@gmail.com

This book is dedicated to . . .

My wife Malinda (Mindy) who in her gentle, consistent way moved me forward, always reminding me of God's purpose, and calling. Her voice can be heard on every page.
My son Matt who first termed the phrase "worshipers who worship."
My daughter Cassie for being the example of a "True Worshiper."
My oldest son Brian, who in the early years, as the idea of the book was beginning, shared many conversations with insight, wisdom, and passion.

My Father has a deep craving for people who actually bow before Him in worship.

—JESUS (JOHN 4:24)

Contents

List of Abbreviations | x

Introduction | 1

PART ONE: DEFINITION OF WORSHIP

CHAPTER 1	HUMANITY'S ASSIGNMENT	5
CHAPTER 2	THE ORIGIN OF WORSHIP	7
CHAPTER 3	WORSHIP, THE WORD	10
CHAPTER 4	THE WORSHIPING SERVANT: GOD'S PRIORITY	20
CHAPTER 5	WORSHIP TECHNICALITY	25
CHAPTER 6	LEGALISM	29
CHAPTER 7	PRAISE OR WORSHIP	31
CHAPTER 8	THE PROCESSION OF PRAISE	36
CHAPTER 9	WORSHIP AND THE GATHERING OF SAINTS	40
CHAPTER 10	THE RECIPE FOR WORSHIP	43
CHAPTER 11	HOW DOES GOD FEEL ABOUT WORSHIP?	47
CHAPTER 12	WHAT DID JESUS DO?	49
CHAPTER 13	WHAT SHOULD WE DO?	51

PART TWO: STORIES OF WORSHIP

The Silent Man | 55
Covert Operations | 58
Backdraft | 60
Fuming Bees | 62
Worshiping God's Way | 64
The Warrior Versus the Commander | 66
Seven Miracles | 69
A Strange Sight | 71
The Master of the Harvest | 73
A True Worshiper | 75
The Cost | 77
Troubled Times | 79
The History of Worship | 81
The Bystander, Part One | 83
The Bystander, Part Two | 84
The Answer | 86
The Grand Opening | 89
Contagious Worship | 92
True Revival | 94
An Age-Old Problem | 96
Too Much Advice | 98

The Transparent Man | 100
The Peaceful Solution | 102
The Peaceful Solution, Part Two | 104
Awaken My Love | 106
Kings and Princes | 109
Scarecrows in a Cucumber Field | 111
Dare to Hope | 113
A Glimpse of the Future | 115
The Last Song | 117
A Muddy Field | 119
The Last Days | 121
The Dysfunctional Family | 123
An Old Battle | 125
Worship 101 | 127
A Simple Plan | 130
The Lost City | 133
Casting Out an Image | 135
Rooftop | 137
A Short Memory | 139
Getting It Straight | 141

The Vow | 143
The True Gift | 147
The Flock | 149
Shoreview | 151
A Talented Mom | 154
A Drowsy Spirit | 157
A Short Sprint | 159
Bad Eggs | 161
The Strong Wind | 163
A Prestigious Guest | 165
Perfect Sight | 167
The Story of Stephen | 169
The Journey | 172
The Journey 2 | 174
The Simple Lesson | 176
The Gathering | 178
Temples and Idols | 180
Our Spiritual Mother | 182
Too Much to Think About | 184

Every Knee (not just a few) | 186
Syncretism | 188
Lost Gods | 190
The Lawless One | 192
A Good Translation? | 194
In Other Words | 196
Living Proof | 198
The Home Church | 200
One Last Time | 202
Faithful Trust | 204
High Praise | 206
Adultery | 208
If | 210
Follow My Instructions | 212
The Truth | 214
The Contender | 216
The Letter Carrier | 218

Conclusion | 220
Bibliography | 221

List of Abbreviations

OT

Genesis—Gen
Exodus—Exod
Leviticus—Lev
Numbers—Num
Deuteronomy—Deut
Joshua—Josh
Judges—Judg
Ruth—Ruth
1 Samuel—1 Sam
2 Samuel—2 Sam
1 Kings—1 Kgs
2 Kings—2 Kgs
1 Chronicles—1 Chr
2 Chronicles—2 Chr
Ezra—Ezra
Nehemiah—Neh
Esther—Esth
Job—Job
Psalms—Ps (Pss when citing multiple chapters at once)
Proverbs—Prov

Ecclesiastes (or Qoheleth)—Eccl (or Qoh)
Song of Solomon—Song
Isaiah—Isa
Jeremiah—Jer
Lamentations—Lam
Ezekiel—Ezek
Daniel—Dan
Hosea—Hos
Joel—Joel
Amos—Amos
Obadiah—Obad
Jonah—Jon
Micah—Mic
Nahum—Nah
Habakkuk—Hab
Zephaniah—Zeph
Haggai—Hag
Zechariah—Zech
Malachi—Mal

List of Abbreviations

NT

Matthew—Matt	1 Timothy—1 Tim
Mark—Mark	2 Timothy—2 Tim
Luke—Luke	Titus—Titus
John—John	Philemon—Phlm
Acts—Acts	Hebrews—Heb
Romans—Rom	James—Jas
1 Corinthians—1 Cor	1 Peter—1 Pet
2 Corinthians—2 Cor	2 Peter—2 Pet
Galatians—Gal	1 John—1 John
Ephesians—Eph	2 John—2 John
Philippians—Phil	3 John—3 John
Colossians—Col	Jude—Jude
1 Thessalonians—1 Thess	Revelation—Rev
2 Thessalonians—2 Thess	

Introduction

My motivation for writing this book came from an unexpected encounter. I say unexpected because at a time when I thought I was doing what I was called to do as a worship leader, musician and pastor, I suddenly became aware of a missing piece. I found myself relentlessly thinking about my title of "worship leader." There were times when I could not sleep at night without the echoing refrain of "What is worship?" bouncing back and forth in my mind.

The process was long, twenty years-plus. It included conversations with pastors, other worship leaders, and close friends and family. It was staggering at times. The book, as small as it is, was written over and over, added to, deleted from, critiqued by men with Ph.Ds. in theology and pastors with longevity behind the pulpit.

My forty years of expertise and experience in composing music, producing, songwriting, and leading praise, coupled with a master's degree in worship studies, would seem to be enough to complete a teaching on worship. That was problem: there was too much. It all came down to the words Jesus said in John 4:24: "My Father seeks, longs for, has a hunger for people who will actually worship Him, His way."

What could I say to that?

Part One

DEFINITION OF WORSHIP

Chapter 1

HUMANITY'S ASSIGNMENT

Then Jesus told him, "Go away, Satan! Because it is written, 'You must worship the Lord your God and serve Him only.'"

—MATT 4:10

IN Matt 4:10, Jesus, prior to entering the work of his ministry, announces that worshiping God, and the service that accompanies it, is humanity's assignment; to be worshipers who serve is the call. Many of us have found God's various service assignments for our lives. Equally important is the discovery of the ministry of worship. To be called a worshiper sounds simple, but is it? Like the mission of service, which comes from heaven's designated plan, worshiping God, God's way, begins with a heavenly design. Do we know what that is?

Today, there is a widespread belief among Christian communities that say every portion of our lives is an expression of worship. The common phrase, "Everything we do is worship," permeates church gatherings everywhere. Contrary to this catchphrase, not

Part One: Definition of Worship

everything we do in daily life, regardless of our intention to serve God, is an act of worship. It would be less stressful to simply ignore this notion. Nonetheless, having encountered God, knowing him personally, we cannot forgo our responsibility to present his word accurately.

Being students of scripture, we accept the fact that we are on a life journey with him, and there will always be something new to learn, regardless of age or past religious experience. An early example of this is found in The Book of Job, chapter 47 (the last chapter). Job comes to the realization that the process of knowing God is ongoing. He says, "I had only heard about you, but now I see you." God responds by saying that his servant Job delivered his word accurately, and because of this, all of Job's prayers would be answered and his friends would be blessed. It is for this reason that an effort is made to deliver God's word accurately when studying worship. Undoubtedly, all of us want our prayers to be answered, as well as our family and friends to be blessed. Therefore, when studying God's word, fastidiousness is important, which is a big word that means "being correct." We can know the truth about worship because heaven's dictionary is in our hands, we only need to be diligent. For those of us who are drawn to worship, heaven's perspective is an asset. The goal is to be aligned with worship as it is in heaven, worshiping God, God's way. So, we start from the beginning.

Chapter 2

The Origin of Worship

Searching out the origin of worship must begin with referencing the word's etymology in the dictionary, which comes from what is known as Old English. In the Old English language, the early spelling of worship was "Worth-Ship."[1] This simply means to honor someone or something in some form or fashion. This earthly explanation of worth-ship, now worship, is a sliver of a thought, far from the heavenly description that we read about in scripture. The worth-ship that comes out of respect of another man's riches, talents, or accomplishments is ashes compared to worship that is offered to the one and only creator, God.

God is worthy of it all, but the definition of worship in today's vernacular does not make room for God's full supremacy. Modern language, combined with Christian doctrine, as well as postmodern traditions, have created a theology of worship. These doctrines have born within the Christian community a belief system that misrepresents heaven's presentation of worship. Over the centuries, the word worship has lost its identity. In place of its heavenly designed response to God's awesome power and greatness, we follow an outline, a prescribed service labeled worship.

1. Cornwall, *Let Us Worship*, 48.

Part One: Definition of Worship

In the book of John, chapter 4, Jesus brings to our attention a new/old concept: *True Worship*. The word that Jesus uses in John 4 is not worth-ship according to old English. What Jesus describes is derived from heaven itself, giving us a picture of our worship heritage, a heritage born not of this earth. The verse that establishes this heritage is found in the following scripture. It begins in the book of Neh.

> You alone are the Lord. You made the heavens and all the stars. You made the earth and the seas, and everything in them. You preserve them all, and the angels of heaven worship him. (Neh 9:6)

Before the heavens and stars, the earth and the seas, angelic beings worshiped God in heaven. Nehemiah reveals the origin of worship. Worship was taking place as God was in the process of creating the universe. The universe was in a state of change, yet worship was a constant. Worship was activated at a time when the earth was not yet in existence. This leads me to believe that the act of worship is firmly rooted in heaven's culture, older than creation itself. This is far from a manmade effort to satisfy an earthly spiritual need. Heaven-designed worship is much more elevated than a religious service entrenched in a selected, human perspective of common liturgy, modern or emerging church theology. In The Book of Neh, the word worship is the same word used throughout the entire Old Testament, and it is the same word that Jesus uses in the book of John chapter 4, with the additive of the Greek language. Not only is the word used at the beginning of creation, it describes worship in The Book of Rev at the end times. That is why I say, worship is a constant.

The act of worship that is found in the heavens, God is looking for, waiting for and craving from his creation, even today, right now. We know by reading Heb 13:8 that God is the same yesterday, today and forever. Like God himself, worship is relentless. The word itself does not change, nor can it be altered to suit a philosophy or theology, lifestyles, or worldviews. Worship can be called true when it is presented to God according to his blueprint. This

The Origin of Worship

heavenly designed blueprint of worship can be found throughout scripture and examined through the definitions that God offers to us in his word. It is these words that define for us the act of worship itself, what it is, when it happens, and with whom. When we understand heaven's vocabulary, we are most likely to worship God, God's way. The key is to see worship through God's eyes, seeing his perspective as we cultivate our terminology of worship.

Chapter 3

Worship, the Word

When reading God's word, various themes are present. In these themes, the predominant thread is worship. Angelic hosts cry out, "Worship him! Worship him!"

All the while, people are saying, "We are! We are!"

When reading the historical journey of the Hebrew nation, we see the people of God replace the act of worship for something else, something manmade. God makes it clear, yet their eyes are murky. When it comes to true worship, there is a blind spot in the human spirit, hindering people from grasping what God is wanting. Here lies the problem.

In the Old Testament, the act of worship was familiar; still, their stubborn hearts ruled them. Failing, they worshiped God in a way that pleased themselves. People, whether they consciously know it or not, have their own personal theology about worship. A woman once said to me that the church where she attends worships God in many ways. That said to me, everyone does it according to their own personal twist. It reminded me of the people of Israel—a past generation of children found in the wilderness. Worship traditions are passed on to each generation. This generation today is developing a new tradition of worship based on self-acceptance and personal preference.

Worship, the Word

Not only is the word worship misused, it has evolved into a product born out of a world of social media. People say, "That is the way worship is: it is many things, you have to accept it for what it is." No! You do not have to accept anything not found in heaven's fields.

The phrase "Worship and Praise" has found its place in nearly every home in America: it's being broadcast on the airwaves, used in television marketing, and in advertising. It is heard or seen on every screen, hanging on the walls of our homes and on the screens in the palm of our hands. On every continent, in each country of the world, we have watched as Christians stand behind microphones singing worship songs. The image cast to the public is not a true depiction of worship. The Christian world is teaching through widespread media that worship is something other than what is found in heaven. They speak the word, worship, but visually promote something else. People say one thing but do another.

Here is an example. I know that an orange is not an apple, because that is what I have been taught. However, when I was young, if someone would have said an orange is an apple, I would have believed it. There would be no reason not to; I would have adopted the word without question. Today, if I were to publicly declare that an apple is in truth an orange, I would be looked at as needing some serious help. This is the equation we find today when describing worshipers who worship. When speaking about worship, they reference singing, song lists, musical style or genre, preaching, teaching, evangelism and so on. To many people, just congregating in a fellowship hall is an act of worship. Depending on who you ask, worship can be nearly anything, if the person's motives are honorable. This is incorrect epistemology. Their definitions are the wrong choice. The goal then, is to clarify the foundational meaning of the word worship.

The following is a short story to illustrate.

In Dan 3:15, three men had been ordered to bow down and worship a dreadful king. The men refused. Standing before a furnace, they are told that when the music stops, they are to bow down or face a horrific death. When the music stopped, one of the

11

Part One: Definition of Worship

men jumped to the front, shouting, "Hold on! I have money. I have saved a percentage every month, and it is a lot. I will give it to you to assist your kingdom."

The king rolled his eyes and said, "I don't need that!"

"Wait!" The second man pushed the other aside. "Would you consider my wheat and grain, all the offerings that I have? My offerings will tell of your greatness!"

The king chuckled beneath his breath, shaking his head. "Your offerings cannot praise me enough," the king murmured.

The last one drew the air deeply into his lungs as he pushed his friends aside. "I have a gift for singing. Listen to my voice, just once, it will satisfy your need for worship."

Seeing the look on the king's face, one of the others joined him. "I have a good voice, too. Pick any song, I know them all!"

The king raised his hand, his brow tightening. "No! No! And no! I have the best musicians in all my kingdom, I don't want a song. I want you to bow down and worship me!"

That is not how this story goes, of course; the three men stood in horror before a burning furnace looking at their fate, refusing to bow down before the king. If this story took place today, I could imagine someone crying out, "Take my song; isn't that worship?" Nebuchadnezzar knew the definition for the Hebrew word for worship, and it was not singing, not offerings, and not presenting money.

Worship is built upon one Hebrew word: "SHACHAH."[1] Throughout scripture, this word describes worship as *the act of bowing one's self to the ground*. First used in Gen 22, Abraham bowed before God in acknowledgment of his promise. The word is used again in Genesis 24, when Abraham's servant finds a wife for Abraham's son. In the Old Testament books, whenever the correct word for worship is used it is Shachah: "Bowing."

Within today's contemporary Christian world, the act of bowing on the ground during a worship service is not denied, but it is highly uncommon. Christians acknowledge the word and the expression, but few make it an actual occurrence. In many places

---

1. Cornwall, *Let Us Worship*, 49.

in the Old Testament, lying on the ground is found as an act of worship associated with a manifestation of a Godly encounter. Could it be that we need a God encounter?

Shachah, bowing face down, for the Jewish community became a cultural lifestyle[2]. By the first century A.D., it was commonplace for a person to bow before a guest or a friend to honor them. We read several instances in the New Testament of men and women being reprimanded by the disciples and by angels when they bowed before them inappropriately. People are told strictly not to bow before man or angels, because worship itself is for God only (Acts 10:28). Thus, bowing is an act that holds consequences, good and bad. Interestingly, the penalty for bowing before an idol is no less greater than not bowing before God at all.

But what are the consequences for people who say they are worshiping when they are not? This could be the most influential reason to know God's definitive word for worship. We need to bow before Him with purpose! The church cannot afford to worship the way past ancestors worshiped, nor can we excuse ourselves for not knowing God's word concerning the First Commandment, or, just as important, the words of Jesus. To be a true worshiper, we need a fresh revelation of worship.

Could true worship slip through the religious cracks in modern-day Christianity? I hope not. Referring to the book of Hebrews, God is the same yesterday, today and forever, I do not believe he has changed his mind about worship. Worshiping God's way is still a prerequisite for those who call themselves worshipers of God. We need to be aware of popular expressions and frail terminology. Worshiping God is serious. Twenty-first century theoretical ideas, nor personal lifestyles, can define the word. Serving God in our community or building an evolving church meeting does not produce worship.

To go back, worship did not originate here on earth, but found its beginning in the heavens. From there, it was translated into the Hebrew language that we read in the Old Testament. With the progression of history, the definition of worship was strengthened

---

2. Scott, *Jewish Backgrounds of the New Testament*, 67.

Part One: Definition of Worship

by the Greek translation of the word. As Alexander the Great traveled through Asia, advancing his kingdom borders, furthering the lifestyles of Greek society, the word for worship was magnified in a greater sense.[3] In the Greek translation (the Septuagint), the word for worship is *proskyneo*. This translation brings even a greater depth to the word. The Greek word for worship translates to the following:

> Bowing facedown, leaning towards the master as a dog licks his master's hand, kissing towards him.

In centuries past, when a person worshiped an idol, they bowed down, kissing the feet of the image. Today, kissing an idol is associated with some religious institutions, as many confessing Christians kiss statues of saints, pictures, or other religious figures. Some believe this is a form of modern-day idol worship. The definition of worship in the New Testament, Proskyneo, builds on the intimacy associated with the act. Do not miss this: worship is not work, nor does it fall into the category of labor for the purpose of receiving a reward. In John 4:24, Jesus explains in detail what God considers to be real worship. In this verse, he uses the Greek word Proskyneo.

For reference, there are six other words written in the New Testament that are at times translated as worship; however, none are associated with Proskyneo—"bowing before, kissing"—in true worship.

In Luke 7:44–46, a woman, in view of all who were in Simon's home, paints an unforgettable portrait. From the moment Jesus enters, she bows down, emotionally clinging to his feet. Her action consists of bowing, accompanied by tears and kisses, covered by her hair and costly perfume. A thought comes to mind: God King, Jesus, deserves that level of worship, and his father would not want it any other way. Looking at Simon, in Luke 7:36–50, Jesus responds to Simon's criticism by saying, "You did nothing, and I was your guest." The lesson: when worship takes place, there

---

3. Scott, *Jewish Backgrounds of the New Testament*, 117.

is noticeable action and substance. Still, even those close to Jesus, like Simon, can miss it.

During a moment of intimate worship, there is one foundational expression based on two words that define this offering of worship: Shachah and *Proskyneo*. In heaven's reality, there are no other forms of worship besides bowing before the master of heaven, kissing his feet. In our world, humanity's view of worship is dim. We as church leaders convey to churchgoers that serving the church community is itself worship; thus, we put them to work thinking they are working worshipers. By the way, this is not incorrect worshipers do work. However, people believe that there is an intrinsic, holistic expression of worship that requires no physical response at all. These concepts are out of sync with God's vocabulary. To help humanity, Jesus decodes the meaning of true worship in John 4:24. Here, Jesus establishes heaven's design of worship

> But the time is coming—indeed, it's here now—when true worshipers will worship the father in spirit and in truth. The father is looking for those who will worship him that way. For God is spirit, so those who worship him must worship in spirit and in truth. (John 4:23-24)

In this well-known scripture, Jesus, strategically uses the word "true" when connecting the worshiper and worship.[4] In Greek, worshiper is "Proskynetes," the person who worships, and "Proskyneo" is the act of bowing down with a kiss. Jesus states that to be called a worshiper, one needs to worship. A worshiper of God will bow down, extending themselves towards God with the depth of love that could produce a kiss. Agreeing with the words of Jesus takes little effort; it is the relearning of the act, the emotions needed, and the application of the word that brings struggle.

The connecting word that Jesus uses as he unfolds heaven's secrets is the word "true." This word is crucial when developing heaven's view of worship. True in Greek is *alethes*, and it literally means *"not hidden, unconcealed—an actual occurrence."* In addition, this word references that which has not only the name and

---

4. *Vines' Complete Expository Dictionary of New Testament Words.*

Part One: Definition of Worship

resemblance of God, but the real nature, corresponding to the name, in every respect, corresponding to the idea signified by the name. It signifies what is real, true, and genuine. It is opposite to what is fictitious, counterfeit, imaginary, simulated or pretended.[5] What Jesus said was, a worshiper cannot just think about worshiping, or pretend to do it through a ministry, such as by offering praise or standing upright, preaching or teaching, or song leading.[6] Worship is not in the mind. For worship to be true, the essence of the word must be demonstrated, like the woman does in Simon's house. True worship cannot be faked or scammed by someone to get something from God, such as the mother of James and John, the sons of thunder, who wanted something in return for her moment of worship. (See Mark 10:25.) The word "true" contrasts realities with their semblances or appearances. The act of bowing is the reality of the word, they are connected; a true worshiper cannot have one without the other. To say "I am a worshiper, but I do not bow" negates the statement that a person is a worshiper. The word "true" is opposite to what is imperfect, defective, frail, or uncertain.

This is saying that bowing down because of a person's love for God is perfect in its sense and is seen as strength in God's eyes. God sees Proskyneo (bowing down) as strength to the worshiper. In its richest meaning, true worship is courageous and sincere, with no alternative motives. A true worshiper does not bow for the sake of conquering something or winning back something that has been stolen. Worship is not presented for the benefit of the worshiper, but to acknowledge the supremacy of God. The most significant portion of the word "true," in connection to worship, is the evidence that worship is an actual occurrence-actually taking place in real time. To be a worshiper, a person needs to present to God "Alethes" the authentic, tangible manifestation of Proskyneo.

In John 4, as Jesus is ministering to the Samaritan woman, he does not focus on the religious issues of the young woman's life. It is not about the place of worship, the history of the temple, or even

---

5. Strong, NT 228.
6. Cornwall, *Let Us Worship*, 55–56.

the level of faithfulness to God's word that he draws attention to. Rather, Jesus continues to carry the torch for worship as it is found in heaven. Like the Samaritan woman, what has happened to the modern-day church is that the church meeting place has lost its focus on the things that are found in heaven. Jesus knew the power that came from heaven, and he saw the river of life that flowed from true worship.

From the second century onward, church leaders centered their energies on the table of communion and the preaching of the Apostles doctrine[7]. The drive behind the gathering of saints is founded on growth and discipleship and saving the lost. Of course, these ministries mentioned have a high place and purpose, however, they were not designed to be worshiped, nor are they worship themselves. Nonetheless, not being an act of worship does not belittle the ministry of the church. Yet, the church will need to acknowledge that ministry in all its forms is not the actual occurrence of bowing before the throne of God. There is an additional element found in John 4. This is when Jesus emphasizes God's disposition and heart toward people who desire to be worshipers. These are the words "*kind*" and "*seeks*."

. . . For they are the *kind* of worshipers the Father *seeks*."
(John 4:23)

The two words "kind," and "seeks" gives us an insight to what God is looking for.

The word "kind" in Greek is *Istorioutos* = *Toi-u-toss*, in its literal sense, means a specific people, of specific character.[8] Some people are born with a humble heart towards God, and they seem to have no issue with sincerely bowing before the God of creation. Then, there are others who need proof, such as a supernatural spiritual experience, before they fall before God. Such was the case for Paul, and Abraham's servant, and Gideon, who, after experiencing God's prophetic abilities, worshiped in the enemy's camp. Think of that!

7. Elwell, *Evangelical Dictionary of Theology*, 87.
8. Vines Expository Dictionary of New Testament Words.

Part One: Definition of Worship

Whatever the circumstance, it is the character of a man that God, when seeking worshipers, is looking for. Some of us have self-centered qualities, meaning that everything we do has to be about us, our ministries, our theology, our church life, and so on. This is a precarious place, especially if we call ourselves worship leaders. What kind of character do we present when leading a song? Is it a character that is willing to bow and worship God? Or are we too self-conscious to worship, choosing to sing instead? There are many questions we need to ask ourselves if we want to reflect heaven's worship style.[9] Here is a brief illustration. (John 9:38)

A man who had been blind since birth encounters Jesus. Before Jesus has healed his eyesight, the man reveals his specific Istorioutos kind of character, when he says, "Tell me (who the son of man is) so that I may believe in him." Before being healed, he was eager to believe. If Jesus would have told him and done nothing else, he would have accepted it, believed, and worshiped him. But now that he could see Jesus, the man said, "Lord, I believe," and then bowed down, worshiping. God saw the character of a worshiper in this man before healing him. Interestingly, being blind, the man had never seen worship, but he did it without hesitation.

The most important detail is this: God is looking for a person with a true character. He is seeking, with a deep craving, people who will physically worship. This leads us to the second word that Jesus emphasized in John 4. The word "seek," in Greek, the word "*Zeteo.*" The word literally means, God seeks, in order to find out, by thinking about it, meditating on it, and reasoning with us as he studies our lives.[10] God has a hunger for true worshipers, as if demanding it, but instead he waits for us to offer worship with a kiss.

What we find, when looking at worship outside of our own traditional viewpoint, is that Jesus in John 4 is not introducing new ideas about worship, but rather, continuing what had begun in the heavens long before the creation of this planet. During his life on earth, Jesus continued spreading the truth about true worship through his words and his actions. Jesus was a true worshiper!

---

9. Sasser and Cornwall, *Priesthood of the Believer*, 140.
10. *Vines' Expository Dictionary of New Testament Words.*

Worship, the Word

Today, we need to continue where Jesus left off. We can do this by accurately representing worship, worshiping like Jesus did. Worshiping God, God's way.

God looks over the earth, at every generation, every face, every name, every born child, every adult, adolescent and elderly person. He looks among those people, seeking to find something in a person that he himself has created, the kind of person who, in their inward places, have a sense of worship. This sense of worship is not found in every person. I have had pastors tell me that they would not bow down before God. They said, "Why would I bow before a loving father? I do not see his need. Jesus never bowed before his father!"

Nevertheless, God looks through a man's flesh, past his bone and blood. He looks for the person who has a specific quality that would lead him to be a true worshiper. Remember 1 Sam 13:44 and Acts 13:22. The Lord sought for himself a man after his own heart. Then he said, "I have found that David, the son of Jesse, is a man after my own heart, who will carry out all my wishes." God is in the business of searching hearts.

Chapter 4

The Worshiping Servant: God's Priority

The devil said to Him, "I will give you all of this if you will bow down and worship me." Jesus said to him, "Go away, Satan! Scriptures say, 'Worship the Lord your God and serve him only.'"

—Matt 4:9-10

Before Jesus begins his ministry, there is an encounter with the adversary. During this meeting, Jesus lays down the rules, putting in place the priorities of his father. Jesus declares to the world that he worships, (Proskyneo) God, and only does he serve him. This brief encounter confirms God's plan for his creation. God's will, stated by Jesus, is that everyone should bow down before him just as they would make efforts to serve him. Bowing down is an expression of serving.

    This worshiping service was not a human's idea serving a religious purpose, but a heavenly designed response to God's interaction and supremacy. Serving God is a combination of things

The Worshiping Servant: God's Priority

performed on behalf of the gospel message. Yet, few realize that a moment on their face before Jesus is a valuable service to God.[1] Like Mary kissing the feet of Jesus, washing and wiping his feet with her tears and hair, when we bow down before him, that ministry continues. So much emphasis has been put on working in the kingdom and serving the saints and the community for the sake of the gospels that the actual occurrence of serving Jesus as a worshiper has been overlooked. Not only is worship a service to God, it is specific in detail.

> "But the Levitical priests, the sons of Zadok, who kept charge of my sanctuary, when the sons of Israel went astray from me, shall come near to me to minister to me, and they shall stand before me to offer me the fat in the blood," declares the Lord. "They shall enter my sanctuary; they shall come near to my table to minister to me and to keep my charge." (Ezek 44:15–16, NASB)

Here is a picture of God followers standing in God's sanctuary, ministering to him. Note that their physical position is not worship, but serving, as they offered the raising of hands presenting the blood and fat sacrifice.[2] Rom 12:1, we find the reference to this specific ministry.

> So, brothers and sisters, because of God's mercies, I encourage you to present your bodies as a living sacrifice that is holy and pleasing to God. This is your appropriate priestly service. (Romans 12:1, CEB)

In various translations, the word service has been replaced with worship, but in this sense, the history of the text does not imply bowing down. The words "they shall stand" in Ezek indicate an active presentation of a required substance, like an animal or offering. Rom 12:1 is the picture of the person who stands serving at a table as a waiter, waiting to take a person's request. In this case, the waiter is not telling the Lord what to order, he is asking him what he wants, then he waits for the answer. That is the quality of

---

1. Brant, *Ministering to the Lord*, 7.
2. Brant, *Ministering to the Lord*, 8.

21

Part One: Definition of Worship

a successful waiter. Paul, in Rom 12:1, is not referencing bowing down as a worshiper, but rather, a servant waiting to serve his master. Some translations mistakenly mark this as an act of worship, when it is correctly a person standing and presenting God with something that he has asked for.

The main point in this verse is that God wants our attention when we come into his dwelling place. This is the most important premise for worship. Worship in heaven's terms allow a person to be in a position where they can honor the one true God without interruptions. True worship demands more from a person then a programmed service can offer. A worshiper, in the most concentrated sense, if they want to achieve their goal, will have to go beyond the average Sunday morning schedule of events.

Remember Joshua? In Josh 5:13, as he is heading into the battlefield, he encounters the Lord of heaven's armies. Joshua, upon realizing it is God, takes off his battle shoes; falling, he worships. At that moment, the battleground is no longer his concern. He is not holding a book of battle strategies in his hands when he falls to the ground—there is no need. Joshua is in the presence of the Lord, the Lord of the battle, and for the time that it took Joshua to worship, God puts on hold the task, purpose and calling of warfare, as Joshua offers the ministry of true worship.

This scenario makes me believe that when I come to a place of worship, bowing down before God, all spiritual battles are put on hold. What importance does one find in this world's distractions when at the feet of Jesus? How can we worship God, with all our mind, our face to the ground, when our thoughts are focused on a future calamity?

Looking back, when Mary performed her ministry to Jesus, her focus was solely on him. She did not acknowledge those around her despite their comments and criticism. This was her uninterrupted personal ministry before her creator and soon-to-be savior. Worship, heaven's style, is a personal ministry time not subject to earth's atmosphere, catastrophic events, governments, or physical surroundings. When worshipers come into the sanctuary of worship, time loses all meaning, and the Lordship of Jesus is

The Worshiping Servant: God's Priority

preeminent. This worship offering is possible through the blood and the fat that Jesus offered for us at Calvary. Without the death and resurrection of Christ, bowing down would have no meaning. With the death and resurrection of Jesus, true worship comes alive—that is the focus. Focus on this: if we deny bowing before our savior, we bring rejection to the sacrifice offered for us through his blood and broken body. When Satan came to Jesus, his goal was to bring rejection and failure to the cross. If Jesus would have bowed before him, the sacrifice would have been lost. Worshiping God matters; it brings power to the blood and life of Jesus. Failing to become a worshiper will bring the same results to the cross that Satan was trying to achieve when he propositioned Jesus. When Mary fell on the floor at Jesus' feet, she presented a picture to the world, fulfilling the voice of Jesus when he said, "You shall worship only God and him only shall you serve."

In Matt 4:9, there is another important issue. Again, the words used in this verse are key to understanding true worship. In this scripture, Satan uses two words when referring to worship. The first word is the Greek word "*Pipto*" and the second word is "*Proskyneo*."[3]

"If you will bow down (Pipto) and worship (Proskyneo) me."

The first word the devil uses as he tempts Jesus is "Pipto." On the surface, it signifies bowing down or bowing the head. But hidden in this word is destruction and failure. Pipto refers to the idea of descending from a higher place to a lower place, to be cast down from a state of prosperity, to fall from a state of uprightness, to lose authority, no longer having force, to be removed from power by death.

In Matt 4:9, Satan's obvious goal is to dethrone the King of Kings, Jesus. Pipto is like handing kryptonite to Superman. Satan wanted to zap the power out of Jesus, ending his ministry and the world as we know it today. Remember this: faulty worship produces separation between God and man, producing the ultimate distraction. True worship works in just the opposite way. When

3. Vines Expository Dictionary of New Testament Words.

Part One: Definition of Worship

people bow down in worship, with no interruptions, solely focused on the creator, it ushers them into the presence of the Almighty God, equipping them to be worshipers who serve God with purpose and power. There is not one instance in the Bible where those who worship God, his way, experienced failure, but rather, become true overcomers. *Failure does not accompany a worshiper.* I say this with no reference to wealth or substantial gain. Worshiping God has no such promised reward—no one walks away from the altar of God with a purse full of coins for a job well done. If that were so, the altar of worship would be crowded with the clattering sound of heavy pockets. Remembering Moses, Joshua, Gideon, and so many others, we see that strength comes to the one who bows down before God. For example, in 2 Chr 20, Jehoshaphat, after surrendering to true worship, found favor at the altar of worship, not destruction. Knowing this, we must be aware of Satan's subtle use of words. The words *Pipto* and *Proskyneo* are separated by just one word. It was a single word that divided Jesus from defeat or victory. This conjunction "and" disjointed true worship from false worship—we cannot have both. Satan tried to create a smokescreen, with the hopes of hiding heaven's cultivated worship style, and in its place, lead Jesus into a false worship expression.

This is the catch. How do we worship? Is it God's way? Or the world's way? Pipto or Proskyneo?

Chapter 5

Worship Technicality

TECHNICALITY: "*A point of law or small detail of a set of rules: their convictions were overturned on a technicality.*" *The specific details or terms belonging to a particular field: "Technicalities of the game. The decision based only on a specific rule or rules and not on any other consideration."*1

It is a fact: worship has been buried beneath a long list of procedures. These techniques include not just the traditional, or liturgical expressions, but the newer, modern additions that we see in church movements today. Cloaked beneath doctrine and modern genre, true worship has been lost to the technicalities built into these gatherings. Like the women at the well, in John 4, who questioned Jesus on the technical term of worship, many of us have designed our own theology on earthly terms, replacing the heavenly act of worship with a set of personal religious technicalities. What makes something a technicality?

A technicality is formed when a particular field of thought is controlled by terms that define the playing field. This means the details that we choose to define what we do will limit those who participate by the technicalities that are applied. Another way to

---

1. Webster's Collegiate Dictionary.

Part One: Definition of Worship

say this is, our rules or decisions regarding worship and what we say it is, do not take into consideration how God views worship, but rather, our technicalities overrule God's definition, limiting people by doing things the way we want them done.

In the field of law, convicted criminals have been set free on technicalities. This means that the truth was overturned by something less than the truth, and because of it, an unlawful act was excused. In some cases of law, the innocent become imprisoned over a technicality not in their favor. We see how a small detail, when used in a negative way, can create a misleading unfavorable result, affecting people's lives.

Unlike a skilled lawyer, most of us do not see the technicalities of religion that have covered the truth concerning the act of worship. The most atrocious misleading technicality regarding worship is the phrase, "Worship is everything." That phrase has in its very center a set of rules that holistically leads people into thinking God has no defined terms regarding worship. It is a teaching that leads people into the irrational idea that they are offering to God a pleasing sacrifice, when, in heaven's reality, what they are doing does not fit the true representation. If worship is everything we do, then there is no right way or wrong way to worship. This way of thinking is outside the technical terms set up by the lawgiver himself. God is a lawgiver, no way around it. Contrary to heaven's view, our beliefs have opened the door to a neutralizing spiritual nerve gas that has floated from one denomination to the next, deactivating the very encounter that one needs to become a true worshiper. As one man said to me, "I cannot sing, so I must not be able to worship." This proved to me the effects and reality of misinformed technicalities about worship.

In the spiritual sense, technicalities such as this one are evil devices designed to weaken the framework of worship. If the church thinks they are worshiping when they are not, based on their own technicalities, the enemy has achieved its objective. The enemy of the church applauds when people of God are bound by their own set of rules. That was Satan's ploy when he tried to trick Jesus into worshiping him in Matt 4:9-10. If Jesus had concurred,

Worship Technicality

the technicality would have destroyed all that worship stood for and all that worship is, in heaven and earth. This is also the devastation that follows religious manmade worship theology. Jesus said that if we teach our traditions as if they were God's commandments, our words will have no power (Mark 7:3-13). We can, by our own words, make the act of worship ineffective, nullified in a sense. We can invalidate worship. Overturning God's word with our list of rules in the form of technicalities has contributed to the worlds blurry view of true worship. Thus, we have taken the true experience of worship, replaced it with entertaining ingenuity, leaving a generation of churchgoers powerless. They may have wonderful intentions to serve God and man, but no endurance for worship.

To think that every song that we sing is an act of worship is a misleading technicality that people over the centuries have given little thought. If a person cannot sing, are they unable to worship? Listening to a sermon or an anointed teaching is seen as a moment of worship; this, too, is a misleading technicality. What if a person cannot hear the message—are they not worshiping? Of course, singing to God in praise is a wonderful service to the Lord and to the body of Christ, just as teaching and preaching is God's plan for the church; but these acts in themselves are not worship. Prophesying, as we read in 1 Cor 14, is not worshiping, but when it is done correctly, it can lead people to a place of worship. Believing that these ministries are the act of worship is to fall for the oldest trick in the book, which is a misleading technicality interrupting God's way of worship.

❀ ❀ ❀

Like a lawyer who has just won a case, freeing the criminal on a technicality, the lawyer will eventually find himself in the same courtroom, trying the same case again, as the person will most likely be a repeat offender. Technicalities have a way of coming back and repeating themselves. How many times has the church had to regroup and reinvent themselves with the hopes of staying current with modern-day society? Why does the church copy the

Part One: Definition of Worship

world in their presentation, music, and their approach to the message of the gospel?

The answer is this: technicalities are unstable; they change with the tide and when the wind blows, they lean from one side of the fence to the other. This is like the law books we find in our courtrooms, as the technicalities are always being rewritten to conform to modern society. Therefore, true worship, and those who understand what a true worshiper is, are not subject to the technicalities of religion. What Jesus said to the woman at the well in John 4 says it all: "You worship what you do not know." Technicalities found in today's modern worship services have kept many from knowing what true worship is. The phrase "everything is worship" is a technicality that confines the human soul. Instead of being overturned by a technicality, one is placed in bondage to the articles found in the technicalities they themselves have created.

This is why we need to reread the words of Jesus in John 4. Looking at this passage of scripture, we see what Jesus wanted for the woman at the well—he wanted her freed from the technicalities of worship that her forefathers had conceived. These past rules had designed a pattern that led to separation and hatred towards others, and eventually estrangement from their creator, God. The woman at the well made the attempt to use these technicalities to trap Jesus, but in return, he offered her the truth about worship, which was to worship God's way with no constraints.

How can we keep ourselves from being a victim of such a technicality? One way is to personally know true worship. Today, as in the time of Jesus, people have unknowingly and knowingly adapted theologies that do not line up with God's thinking. Misunderstood, poorly translated words have played a part in the erroneous theories about worship, but nothing is more misinterpreted than the phrase, "praise and worship."

Chapter 6

Legalism

Here is something to consider.

Legalism: 1. *Strict, literal, or excessive conformity to the law or to a religious or moral code / the institutionalized legalism that restricts free choice1.*

People do not like being forced to do something. They cherish free choice. Whether believing in, or having a relationship with Jesus, God, or the Holy Spirit—they want to do things their own way. 2 Cor 3:27 says, "Now the Lord is the Spirit, and where the Spirit of the Lord is, there is freedom." That is more than a good motto. Christians are not bound, chained, or tied in any way to the sinning nature of this world. We are covered by the blood of Jesus, and that covering allows us freedom to overcome this world even in the face of death (Rev 12:11).

However, God has an opinion about free choice. He is also a lawgiver. He has a code of conduct, integrity, and ethics. Read Apostle Paul's letters to the church. God's code is in the defined term of legalism, in the most powerful sense. Legalism in God's world offers benefits to mankind—lifesaving benefits.

---

1. Webster's Collegiate Dictionary.

Part One: Definition of Worship

When we think of legalism, we often see the bad side, but there is a good side. Example: to say there is only one way to heaven makes people angry. The world does not like to hear that Jesus is the only way. They see that as legalistic and unfair. There are a few more "One Ways" that we need to consider. Love is one. It must be unconditional for it to have power (1 John 2:15). If we want the love of the father in us, we cannot love this world. Powerful legalism. Matt 20:16, "So, the last will be first, and the first will be last." True legalism. Matt 10:39, "Whoever finds their life will lose it, and whoever loses their life for my sake will find it." Living legalism. Jesus, in John 4:24, "God is Spirit, and His worshipers *must* worship Him in spirit and in truth." Legalistic worship. The word "must," small and unnoticed, needs to be noted, meaning "it is necessary." Legalism is a truth. It is necessary to bow down to be a true worshiper. Even in that, some will say, "You are being legalistic." God's legalism breathes life at the altar of worship.

Chapter 7

Praise or Worship

When unraveling the misconceptions of worship, it is advantageous to have a grasp of the purpose and spiritual meaning of praise. Our culture has mixed beliefs when using these two words, and because of that, clarification would benefit the believer who is interested in worshiping. One of many reasons why praise is so important is that it finds its expression within the setting of the congregation of God. Praise needs to arise from the mouth of the saints, spontaneously, so to give God a place of habitation (Ps 22:3).

Prior to the twentieth century, the words "praise and worship" were not used in the same sentence. Willian Booth a British Methodist preacher, the founder of the Salvation Army, clearly defined praise and worship as two separate responses to God[1]. In the Bible, the two words were seldom linked together. One of the most well-known verses is found in The Book of Acts, chapter 16, Paul and Silas are imprisoned. Here we see Paul bowing down, worshiping, while singing praise to God. For the first time in the New Testament, worship and praise is found in the same verse. Today, the slogan, "worship and praise" is found everywhere; even people who do not believe in God or know Jesus personally have

---

1. McDow and Ried, *Firefall*, 271.

Part One: Definition of Worship

most likely heard the catchphrase. If praise and worship is indifferent, something is missing. Either praise is worship, or worship is praise. As a side note: Becoming more popular than "praise and worship" is just the phrase "worship," as many are now leaving out the mention of praise, as if it is all the same.

It comes back to this: Jesus says in Matt 15:9, "In vain do they worship me. Their teachings are only human rules." In the Living Translation Bible, the verse sounds like this: "Their worship is a farce, for they teach manmade ideas as commands from God." Jesus is saying, if our language is not God's language, and we act as if it is, we make our lives ineffective, and our worship becomes powerless doctrine and frail speech. Do not be mistaken, Jesus understood praise. In Luke 10:21, Jesus was dancing and rejoicing in the streets. Jesus sang (Matt 2:30), lifting his hands (Luke 24:50) towards heaven. He also worshiped, bowing down (Luke 5:16). Jesus did not send mixed messages concerning worship and praise. So, why do we?

Praise and worship have their own specific characteristics. Praise fulfills the personal need that God has for his people, individually, as well as the corporately. We see its purpose, for instance in Ps 84:2, where David longs for God's presence during the corporate gathering of the people of God in the outer courts of the Sanctuary, the place where praise is front and center. While worship, even when seen in scripture at times as a corporate offering, is an individual act. Praise is often found under supervision by choir directors and orchestra leaders, while worship has no need for a director, other than the Holy Spirit. Praise extends the parts of the human anatomy upwards in a display of God's glory, while worship humbly folds the physical man downward out of human view. Praise is boldly triumphant; worship is complete surrender. Praise announces God in a prophetic voice, worship bows in silent holiness. Praise is contained in seven Hebrew words, while true worship is embraced by one word. Praise is often demonstrated by those who are skilled; worship needs nothing but a heart that has no doubt. Praise is contingent on strength; worship is best offered by those who are weak. Praise reflects victory, while bowing in worship is not contingent on earthly benefits.

The most basic reason for identifying the differences between praise and worship is this: if a person thinks praise is worship, that person will most likely enjoy the courts of Lord as the inner portions of the temple, the holy place goes unnoticed. The position that Mary found herself in, they will never know. This mishap has at its root Satan's ploy against God. Satan has always wanted worship for himself and will be content if the church remains satisfied with praise, relinquishing worship altogether. There is no better way for Satan to achieve this than by telling people that praise and worship are the same thing. The following is a list of words for praise and its comparison with worship.

Praise (Hebrew Words)[2]

Towdah = the sacrifice of praise with the lifting of the hands.

Yadah = power praise with all strength, throwing out the hands as if throwing a stone.

Zamar = to touch the strings with excitement. Playing a musical instrument.

Barak = quietly bowing the head.

Tehillah = spiritual spontaneous songs inhabited by God.

Halal = clamorously foolish celebration.

Worship (Hebrew/Greek)[3]

Shachah/Proskyneo = bowing down, as a dog licks the master's hand, kissing with affection.

In the expressions of praise, the person finds themselves lifting their hands, playing musical instruments, quietly resting with head tilted downward, shouting, dancing, and rejoicing with great joy, singing spiritual guided songs. In worship, one expression is shared by two words, bowing down with affection. Of course, the worshiper could be singing, joyful and quietly waiting, lifting their hands; however, worship comes alive when the person is in a prostrate position, while the one who offers praise stands in full view "showing forth their praise" (1 Pet 2:9 NKJV). The words for Praise

---

2. Sasser and Cornwall, *Priesthood of the Believer*, 83–98.
3. Cornwall, *Let Us Worship*, 51.

Part One: Definition of Worship

are the tools used to create the spiritual offerings. To worship, a worshiper will lay their tools down, bowing before their Creator.

Some time ago, my wife and I went to an evangelical outreach at a local university in Southern California. The meeting was held in an open, grassy area, surrounded by twisting and turning sidewalks with high-rise student housing on all sides. There was a stage, lights, PA system—all that is needed to have an outdoor event. A short introduction, and the praise music began. Forty-five minutes later it ended, and a DJ came center stage and introduced all the players in the band, giving each one an ovation of thanks before beginning his portion of the evening outreach.

Intermittent music was played by the DJ, filtered with funny jokes, as several hundred gathered center stage, shouting and jumping as the talent moved them. From where I was standing, I watched the crowd bopping up and down, shouting slogans in response to the Christian DJ leading, throwing outstretched hands into the air. The more the DJ invested himself, the more people reacted. The energy was noticeable. There were also people standing on the fringes, onlookers. It was dark by then, and I could not see expressions. Most were talking to one another, while glancing at the tightly packed group center stage.

Then, unexpectedly, my eye caught something. A black outline. A dark silhouette. I could see it was a woman. First, I thought she needed help. Perhaps she had fallen or fainted. Within moments, laying face down on the concrete sidewalk, in the middle of the spectators, her arms stretched forward, her hands pointing straight. Amid the crowd, in the shadow of night, a worshiper emerged. People walked around her, some stepped over her. She remained still. I do not know how long she was there. I did not approach her. Glancing from the crowd, and then to her on the ground, the Holy Spirit reminded me—worshipers are most often found outside the crowd, beyond center stage, not wanting recognition and like worship itself, they go unnoticed.

Here is another example: let us take the phrase, fasting and prayer. A person can be fasting while not engaging in prayer, and prayer is certainly not contingent on fasting. Many assume that

Praise or Worship

because a person says they are fasting that they are also submerged in deep prayer. What is true is that both words work well together and are often found in similar verses. Fasting sharpens the senses of prayer, and the words prayed during a time of fasting are more focused. So is the case of praise and worship. Extended times of praise can lead to an open expression of worship, and worship can draw the heart into a meaningful time with praise. The popular example is Paul and Silas, when in prison (Acts 16:25). Paul worshiped (bowing down while praying) as he offered praise, singing spiritual songs. The combining of ministries is not an issue. God has no difficulty in mixing and matching ministries and callings. Again, the problem lies with us. We need to realign ourselves with God's heavenly perspective. Bowing down and singing are acceptable acts of praise and worship.

Chapter 8

THE PROCESSION OF PRAISE

(SEE: 2 SAM 7:6, 1 CHR 13–16, PS 68:25–27)

GOD's people are joyfully strong when they find their place in the procession of praise. Leaders, joined by singers, musicians, dancers, and those who can rejoice, together create a pageant of expressive sound. This sound has a destination, a purpose for existing, a framework. When combined with the words of praise, this musical demonstration produces a passionate public display of human expression this world has seldom heard. 2 Sam 7:6, 1 Chr 13–16, and Ps 68:25–27 tell a story of this procession of praise.[1]

The framework is like a parade. There are God believers in the front, middle and rear. Everyone is heading in the same direction, following the same tune, freely expressing themselves in different ways. For example: singers sing, instrumentalists play, dancers dance, drummers drum, those who rejoice do it with all their strength. The objective is to move as a group, all traveling together in unity. The procession has a starting place, then ending at Zions Hill, the highest place where God in his fullness is waiting.

1. Conner, *Tabernacle of David*, 69–77.

The Procession of Praise

This, of course, is the short synopsis, a limited version—there is far more to say about the procession of praise and its journey into the presence of God. What is important to underscore is worship is not present in this procession. Every offering, even the animal sacrifices offered every six steps (see 1 Chr 13-16), is a free-will praise offering, standing and waving the portion of the sacrifice in the air before the Lord. This is a journey of praise, not a voyage of worship. The journey of the Ark (God's presence) has many lessons, but worship is not one of them.

Throughout history, this procession of praise has surfaced above the waves of humanity many times. In Exod 15:20, Miriam, tambourine in hand, is followed by other women in a prophetic parade after escaping the Egyptians. In Judg 11:34, Jephthah's daughter meets him with tambourine, dancing—a small, joyful procession. When Jesus entered Jerusalem, there was a massive procession of praise waiting for him, ushering him into his kingdom.

In later centuries, men such as John Calvin, John and Charles Wesley, James McGready, Charles Grandison Finney, DL Moody, Billy Sunday, and Billy Graham, not to mention countless others, all experienced a procession of praise at various levels.[2] When the people in France heard for the first-time music being played during communion, John Calvin witnessed a procession of praise. Even though small by today's standards, it was a shocking sound to the world's ears. James McGready, American revivalist, experienced the power of praise when three churches in the southern portion of Kentucky met by three rivers, producing an unbelievable procession of praise, unstoppable at times, leading to a Second Great Awakening. Charles Finney (a song leader himself) institutionalized the use of the procession of praise, building meetings around the soloist who sang above the crowds with no amplification. DL Moody, Billy Sunday, and Billy Graham followed that example with great success.

The procession of praise is built into God's DNA, like it is ours. Today, the procession of praise continues; however, it is not

---

2. McDow and Reid, *Firefall*, 203-75.

Part One: Definition of Worship

recognized as such. Rather, in this generation, the parade of praise has been mislabeled. Praise leaders, like King David, were not worship leaders, but directors of people coming together to praise, walking side by side with the common goal of reaching the Tent of Meeting. This Tent of Meeting was a gathering place at the top of Zions Hill in Jerusalem where the Ark of the Covenant was placed beneath a tent. During the life of Moses, it was known as the tabernacle of Moses, or the Tent of Meeting, Exod 33:7-11. Here the people experienced the presence of God.[3] I am not saying these men from the past were perfect. Not at all. Many of them stopped the procession before it had barely moved a few steps, replacing it with their own ministry talents, doctrines, or denominational traditions, or just following an outline of revival techniques.

I had an opportunity to speak to an eyewitness, a man who when he was a young boy went to Billy Sunday's meetings. He said the songs went on and on. The crowd roared with praise. At the pinnacle of the procession of high praise, Billy Sunday slid out like a baseball player (which he had been) sliding into home plate, then he jumped up and stole the show. His song leader, Homer Rodeheaver, was known to make the comment while leading songs, "Can you believe they are paying me to do this?"[4] Sounds insignificant, but is it?

In contrast, in other movements, such as the Laymen Prayer Revival beginning in 1857, hosted by Jerimiah Lamphier, church leaders had no desire to steal the show, song leaders were not popular icons. Instead, they found themselves waiting on God, following a deep moving procession, being a part of the prairie fire of praise and prayer sweeping across America.

When we find our place in this procession of praise and allow God to do His part, the world sees a powerful demonstration, like in 1 Chr. If we take responsibility for this march of praise, thinking that its success relies on us, reaching up to steady God's vehicle with our talents and callings, we hinder its movement. Like Uzzah, worried that the (Ark) procession will stumble and fall, we cause it

3. Conner, *Tabernacle of David*, 69–77.
4. McDow and Reid, *Firefall*, 288.

The Procession of Praise

to stop. Like the story goes, it took time for the procession to begin again, prolonging the resting place of God's spirit on his people. Stopping the procession of praise is one thing; saying that our time of praise is itself worship goes beyond the plunder of Uzzah.

As leaders in this procession of praise, we often look ahead, sensing the end of the procession. Believing that high praise is the goal, calling it worship, we leave the people with a failed ending to their journey. If the goal is the procession of praise, the journey would be short, as it is in many meeting places. This might sound silly, but there is a pot of gold at the end of the rainbow. When the procession of praise arrived at the Tent of Meeting, the blessings did not stop there. King David displays God's continued mercies as provisions were given to the people who had arrived at Zions Hill. They went home not only tired from participating in the march of praise, but taking with them food for their families, fully satisfied.

When the praise ends, people need to be allowed freedom to wait, worshiping God's way in his presence, granting the Holy Spirit time to distribute gifts to men.[5] This is not a "good job" reward of some kind. What God gives in the moment of worship, is spiritually the manna, water, and oil. As people worship, praise melts away, strength returns to the weak, poor become rich, and people walk away satisfied in him. This is more than just a big bang at the end of a good parade—it is heavier than long shouts to a great song, or an emotion-filled applause. It is God finding the ones he is jealous for, worshipers who have worshiped in spirit and truth, as Jesus described in John 4.

---

5. Cornwall, *Let Us Worship*, 97.

Chapter 9

Worship and the Gathering of Saints

Contrary to our personal church theology, worship is not meant to be the focus of the gathering of saints. That is a shocking statement coming from a prescribed worship leader. The church gathering in the first century did not come together to worship. According to the letters of Paul in 1 Cor 14, the goal of a church gathering is for the purpose of edifying and spiritually strengthening believers and breaking bread (eating). The gathering of saints, as seen in Eph 3:10, has a different calling, which is for the operation of spiritual gifts demonstrated through the saints (2 Cor 14). In Ephesians, Paul states, the reason for this is so God can prove to those in heavenly places that he is on the throne. God is still proving himself—how can that be? You would think that just creating the universe would be enough. If he is still proving himself to those in heaven, where do we stand? What do we need proof of? Worship? What could be more important than that? To achieve this New Testament objective, the gathering place of God's people need to activate the Holy Spirit's gifts. Within this list of specific instructions to the church, worship becomes the overflow of the gifts in operation, not the gift itself. Worship is not a gift that needs

Worship and the Gathering of Saints

operating; it is a privileged choice. This simply means that when a person or persons in a meeting allow the Holy Spirit to distribute his gifts, such as prophecy, the results will be the demonstration of the power of God, leading some into a worship response to his power. Paul did not invent this scenario; he witnessed it firsthand in the meetings he attended in the city Corinth. The goal then, in Cor 14, is not the act of worship, not singing in praise, but the realization that God can be, and wants to be, actively moving in the meeting place through the Holy Spirit's power and gifts.[1] According to Paul, when the secrets in the hearts of men are reveled to them, they fall on their faces in worship, declaring that God is there. We want people to say, "God is really here!" To support Paul's understanding of church gatherings, he continues his instructions to the church in Eph 3:10.

> God's intent was that now, through the church, the manifold wisdom [spirit-led gifts] of God should be made known to the rulers and authorities in the heavenly realms. (Eph 3:10)
>
> ... and thus, are the secrets of his [a man's] heart made manifest, and so falling down on his face he will worship God and report that God is among you. (1 Cor 14:25)

To some of us, this sounds spiritually wonderful, but others doubt. Either way, it leaves the church in a vulnerable state. If the church is not having a genuine encounter with the Holy Spirit, they will find it difficult to experience what I call "Spirit-filled worship." If Paul's instruction regarding the gifts of the Holy Spirit as they apply to the gathering of Saints is sidestepped, the meeting place could become a gathering based on good humanitarian ideas and simple theology, beautifully performed songs and talented Bible reading. Not a bad choice, but not the best choice. Interestingly, the same spirit that is spoken of in Corinthians and Ephesians is the same spirit that Jesus draws attention to in the book of John, chapter 4. True worship is bowing down in the Holy Spirit, not out of a religious liturgical design or work performance of some

---

1. Sasser and Cornwall, *Priesthood of the Believer*, 132.

Part One: Definition of Worship

kind. Jesus, in John 4, does away with the ceremonial aspects of worship, leaving only one expression. This heaven styled worship is connected to the thoughts and will of the Holy Spirit and is the foundation for it. When the body is encouraged through the gifts of the Holy Spirit, people find love, passion and strength leading them into a time of worship. This is the test of the true worshiper.

Chapter 10

The Recipe for Worship

In the book of Matt 12:30, we find a recipe for a relationship with God.

"You shall love the Lord God with all your heart, soul, mind, and strength."

The words in Matt 12:30 are a blueprint for a successful interpersonal experience of worship. If anyone were to apply these four parts of biblical speech to a personal relationship, the relationship would not fail due to lack of commitment. These four pieces and the value that they describe are also the fundamental forces behind God worship. Like Jesus, worship is fully expressed in these capacities and are copiously activated. This means, that when we love God with passion, with our soul, which is the breath within us, and when our thoughts (the pictures we see in our mind) are focused, applying our full strength to the position of bowing, it is then we find the full spectrum of true worship taking place: the whole person worshiping God as a complete offering.

Even though this is a best-case scenario, one does not need these four pieces to be an activated worshiper. What am I saying? A person might not be able to give his or her mind in complete focus as they bow, or their full heart, or strength, but they can still offer themselves in worship as they lay on the ground before God,

Part One: Definition of Worship

giving Him what they have. Hopefully, over time, the person will learn to take their thoughts captive, focusing on God for more than just a few moments. The same applies to the heart, soul, and strength. The goal is to develop the discipline that is needed to be a worshiper, offering all with sincerity. The heart can feel the need to bow, while the mind fights it with pictures of rejection and false humility. Sometimes we are just too tired to bow. It is hard to get up once we are face down. But in the soul, the life in us, the spirit calls out: "Come on body! Let's do this."

Here is a way to visualize this. Try to remember your high school science classroom days and picture an atom. There was a poster on every science room wall, you do remember that? Right! At the center of an atom is a nucleus. Circulating around the nucleus are electrons. These electrons are essential parts to the nucleus; they give it identity. In worship, the nucleus is "Proskyneo": the act of bowing. Revolving around this act are the different electrons, called the heart, soul, mind, and strength. The parts circulating around the nucleus do not change the nucleus itself but give deeper meaning to it. Like the atom, worship sometimes has only a few parts—the heart, or the mind, sometimes just the strength is enough, but again, that does not alter the truth about the center of worship. It is when the act of bowing is taken out of the equation that it ceases to be worship. Like taking the nucleus away from the electrons, there would no longer be the active response from the electrons, and it would disappear. Without the nucleus, there is no atom. Without bowing, there is no worship. Putting anything in the place of Proskyneo (bowing) destroys the spiritual structure.

We can say that we love God with our heart, soul, mind, and strength, and we should, but just admitting to it does not constitute the act. Think about it for a moment. I can be driving in my car thinking about God, loving him for what he has done, while in my soul I acknowledge his existence, yet, if I am going to continue driving my car successfully, it is not a good idea to bow down in the front seat while the car is still moving forward. I would be much more successful if I were to pull over and take a moment. A more intimate example is this: the husband who loves his wife must do

The Recipe for Worship

more than just speak of his affection for her, there must be the action of intimacy to constitute and affirm his adoration, bringing it to reality, the actual occurrence. Plainly, words or thoughts are not enough.

Today, pulling over and stopping the car so we can worship God for a few moments is not something we do in our regular day of events. On a normal day, most of us are in a state of constant motion, moving from one chore to the next. In our Sunday morning worship gathering, our lifestyle bleeds over. We believe that one must be continually in motion for the gathering to be successful and stay on schedule. Song to song, order list to order list, sermon to sermon. There can be no pauses, no moments of waiting as we express our thought of worship in action. To make Sunday a place of worship, those who are in the driver's seat would have to pull over and stop the vehicle long enough to give the passengers a few intimate moments, before pulling out again on the highway of the church gathering journey. It is hard to stop a moving vehicle; one cannot slow it down by putting their foot out the door, sliding it along the pavement, but it can be done through the right channels.

I was speaking to a small group of Christians about worship. The concepts were easily realized, and it appeared that the people were grasping the idea. When the pastor stood to close the service, instead of inviting people to come and worship, he said, "Let us bow in our hearts for a few moments."

Instantly, I thought to myself, *The heart cannot bow unless the body does*. I love God with my heart, but I worship with my being, my body as a whole. That is what Jesus was saying to the woman in John 4. The pastor at that meeting had his foot on the brake, but never pulled over. Remember this story:

A powerful king found himself under a fierce attack. There was no way out of what appeared to be destruction and death. The king called everyone to come to a meeting—women, children, old men, warriors, all of them. It was not a meeting as usual. No format, no structured beginning, no planned ending. No singing, even though all the musicians were there in the front row. For the first time, the king put the brakes on! "I have got nothing!" he

45

Part One: Definition of Worship

admitted to the assembly of God believers. "Not one solution!" he cried.

Then, the Lord's voice rang out. Within milliseconds, the king and all the people bowed down and worshiped. Afterwards, the musicians stood, presenting high praise to the Lord (2 Chr 1-20.) Who ever said songs come before worship? At this meeting, the singing came after.

Chapter 11

HOW DOES GOD FEEL ABOUT WORSHIP?

JUST as important as our belief about worship and what the word means, is how God feels about worship. Does he really care if we bow down or not? In Exod 20:5, we read that God was jealous over worshipers who worshiped the wrong thing. He speaks of carved images of any size, shape, and form. He notes things living, that fly or walk, or swim. He clearly says, "Do not bow down to them, do not serve them in any way because I am a God, the only God, and I am jealous when you worship, bowing down to anything but me."

In John, 4:23, Jesus said that his Father continually craves those who are worshipers. He draws our attention to the future, saying that there is a time coming when true worshipers will worship him in spirit and in truth. He was speaking of a time when people, the church, would experience true worship for what it is. There would come a time when they would catch the spirit behind it, and the truth surrounding it. He also said that the father with his own eyes has a longing for people who are just like that-He is waiting to see them.

In Rev, chapter 11:1, God is so concerned about true worship in the last days that he sends angels to the gatherings of believers and measures the depth of their worship. He gives a measuring rod like a staff to an angel, and he tells the angel to measure the temple of God, counting the number of those who are worshiping. He says nothing about singing, praising or the other things we do when we meet. He does not count how many verses were sung, or how loud the voices were. The sermon is not reviewed or monitored for content. He looks directly at those who are bowing down, worshiping.

We see in Rom 14:10–12, that along with judgment, bowing down accompanies the confession of those who have faith. This tells me that God is yearning for his creation to lay face down on the ground, abandoning themselves, leaning toward him with a love that desires to give God a kiss. In Rom 14 verses 10–12, He discusses the relationships between brothers and sisters and how they treat one another with contempt, and he reminds them that there is a judgment seat, and they will be judged for their contempt towards one another. He also reminds them that he is alive, and that every knee will bow before him. No one is excluded from bowing down and worshiping, as every person's mouth will acknowledge the God of creation. Each one of us will give an account of ourselves as worshipers who confess with our mouth. This is not only a time of confession, but a historical moment of worship being displayed to the heavens.

Chapter 12

WHAT DID JESUS DO?

WHEN I first encountered the life of Jesus, I did not think of him as the deity that I needed to worship. It was the savior portion of Jesus's life that appealed to me. Years later, I saw Jesus as the one that I would worship. The realization that Jesus bowed before his father had a great impact on my life as a worship leader. When I saw Jesus bowing down, giving adoration and honor to God, it created the desire in my heart to do the same. When I lowered myself to the ground, the Lord met me there; his presence was heavy.

For many of us, it is after the first encounter with Jesus that we discover we, too, are a Jesus worshiper. Following the ministry of Jesus, we find him not only serving in his ministry, but also drawing away from the work to fulfill his ministry of a worshiper. Luke chapter 15 verse 16 says this: "That Jesus often, in the course of the day, withdrew to bow down before His Father." The word used in this verse is the one that combines bowing and speaking out thoughts with love.

In Matt 26:39, we see Jesus falling quickly with intent, as he bowed his face on the ground, worshiping God's way. With these pictures in mind, I have no doubt that worship was an actual occurrence in the life of Jesus.

Part One: Definition of Worship

Not only does Jesus define what worship is in heaven, he gives the world an image of God's expectations for those who call themselves worshipers. If we are brave enough to wear the wristband that says, "What would Jesus do," we should be willing to worship our father like Jesus did. In Heb chapter 12, it points out that we have come to Mount Zion, the heavenly Jerusalem. Again, it is the reality of heaven that we cling to.

Chapter 13

WHAT SHOULD WE DO?

WE have sung the words to this song many times: "Let us worship and bow down", "we bow down, we lay our crowns." There are many more songs that we sing that underscore the invitation to worship. As song leaders, we have shouted from the platform "Come join us in worship!" We announce to the congregation, "Come and bow down with us," yet we stand, singing loudly. It is right that we invite them, but then again, shouldn't't we participate with them as well?

Throughout his life, Jesus made time for worship. He scheduled it into his daily planner, and when he heard his father calling, he dropped his work, making time for Holy Spirit-led worship. If all we have is two hours a week together, shouldn't't we schedule an hour for worship? Why not bow before our creator together during a worship service? I promise you God will not be offended.

Knowing something about the human condition, comfort is man's worst enemy. Yet, we have made the meeting place of God, a God-like lounge, a spiritual comfort zone, all within our own reason. Why would anyone lay themselves face down on the floor, when they have in front of them a soft chair, coffee, tea, and wonderful music filling their ears? Of course, they might if they understood what it meant to worship Jesus, God's way.

Part One: Definition of Worship

Like all things Jesus asks us to do, there is a price for being a worshiper. This worship concept is problematic for all of us. The easy answer could be to remove the word itself and call the service something else other than a "worship time." A celebration, a song service, the teaching hour, something that does not have the word "worship" attached to it, would be much safer. It is a feeble idea to announce to the world that you are a worshiper, and then deny it. If you are convinced, like I am, you can find a place anywhere and bow yourself before God; it does not have to be in a church gathering—a watering hole would be sufficient. Remember, Gen 24:48, Abraham's servant, overwhelmed by the discovery of God's provision, bows himself, worshiping in a watering hole, feet, hands and face covered in mud.

If the church does not worship by heaven's design, who will? If we do everything God's way, except for worship, what is that saying to the hosts of heaven, who are constantly watching? What effect will our worship have on the people of this earth who have no idea what true worship is? Why did the Psalmist say these words?

"Come, let us bow down in worship, let us kneel before the Lord our maker." (Ps 95:6).

Part Two

STORIES OF WORSHIP
From Genesis to Revelation

The Silent Man
A Worship Story based on Gen 17

When Abraham was ninety-nine years old, the Lord appeared to him. He said to Abraham, "I am God Almighty. Live in my presence with integrity. I will give you my promise, and I will give you very many descendants." Immediately, Abraham bowed with his face touching the ground.

—Gen 17:1–3

God said to Abraham, "Don't call your wife by the name of Sarah anymore, instead, her name is Sarah [princess]. I will bless her, and I will also give you a son by her. I will bless her, and she will become a mother of nations, and kings will come from her." Immediately, Abraham bowed with his face touching the ground. He laughed as he thought to himself, "Can a son be born to a one-hundred-year-old man? Can Sarah, a ninety-year-old woman, have a child?"

—Gen 17:15–17

Comfortably, he sat alone in his tent, a robe over his shoulders, a smoldering fire at his feet. From where he rested, he heard children as they raced past, making the noises children make when having fun. Mixed in with voices of children, men and women worked, carrying jars of water, leading camels and sheep. It was a busy place now. Shifting his weight, he tried to get comfortable. It was not an easy task, because his bones were deeply tired, and they would ache. Servants brought him his favorite food, but he was not hungry, not like he was after a long day of hard work. For him, the workday was long past. Now Abraham's job was to rest and remember. With each day, he thought of his Princess, the mother of his children. He pictured her beautiful face, as if she were young, still sleeping in his tent. His Princess had gone to sleep years ago, and there was not a moment that he did not miss her. It was through her child that the promise came; the child he nearly struck down. The memories now fading, it was bits and pieces, but it was enough. He thought, *How, could anyone remember all of it?* The years between children, the families that married under his tent, and the vows of promise. It was impossible to count them, for they had become like the grains of sand on the beach. Shifting only his eyes, faintly, he looked at the walls of his dwelling. The walls that first were small, now were larger, too large to manage. *I lived with integrity, always aware of the presence of God, I do remember that,* he thought to himself. Pulling the blanket up and over his shoulders, he thought, *He promised me nations, I see them now.* Scratching his head, he smiled. Still thinking to himself. *There are so many I cannot count them all.* So many kids. His eyelids slowly shut, then opened again. He did not keep track of time. There was no need to. "I did laugh. Didn't I?" He said out loud. His eyes rolled toward heaven, "I meant no disrespect, Father. I would bow down now if I could, but I would need someone's help to get up again."

THOUGHT EXERCISE

List the promises that you have in Christ. How many are there? Like the grains of sand on the beach, are there too many to count? If you have none, perhaps you have not looked hard enough. How many times has God spoken something extraordinary into your ear at a time when you were not expecting it? Can you count those? If

The Silent Man

none, perhaps you are not accustomed to his voice, yet. How many times have you bowed down on your face before God? Can you count those? If you have not bowed because of his promises, what about because of his greatness, his majesty, his wonderful love offered to you through his son? If you think age has something to do with it, remember Abraham—he was nearly one hundred years old when he bowed in his home, worshiping God. We should all bow down before we get old and forget or need someone there to help us get up.

Covert Operations
A Worship Story based on Gen 24

BEHOLD, Rebecca is before you, take her, and go, and let her be the master's son's wife, as the Lord had spoken. And it came to pass, that, when Abraham's servant heard their words, he worshiped the Lord, bowing himself to the earth. (Gen 24:51–52).

The mission was to travel across hostile territory, carrying gifts and jewelry worth thousands of dollars, with the hope of finding an unknown woman who would accept the proposition. The servant chosen to accomplish this high-level covert operation had doubts that he would succeed. His master, however, knew and feared the one true God, having faith to believe he would return successful. Nonetheless, the servant traveled far with a heart of disbelief. Then, at his arrival, everything suddenly took a turn. Effortlessly, the assignment ended as the women appeared and the proposal was accepted. Moments later, the jubilant servant publicly responded to his success in an unexpected fashion. Bowing facedown, in the watering hole of camels, the faithful servant worshiped Abraham's God for the first time. Intimate worship-mission complete.

THOUGHT EXERCISE

For some of us, it takes more than a word of promise; it takes an out-of-the-ordinary act of God before we fully understand true worship. We walk the walk, serving the master each day, but for many of us, it is not until the supernatural takes place that we fall before God in worship. Bowing in front of all while seeing only one is the goal, and like many things that the master requires of us, bowing down in public among the working class in broad daylight can only be borne out of a true miracle of God. However, as we follow the master's directions, going out in faith to complete a mission, we see the mission objective is but a small part of the creator's strategy. In this story, the servant believes that finding the secret maiden is the sole purpose of his mission. God, however, knows the master's son's soulmate lives; he sends her to the well at just the precise moment. So, is this the climax of the story, the woman coming to the well? Or, was it the treasure handed over to Laban, that we should mark for future reference?

Perhaps, the get-rich story of the once-poor girl now made a millionaire. Again, was the moral of the story another example of Abraham's long faith walk with his God and his ability to hear God's voice? It could be all of these, but it could also be more than the obvious. After countless steps of dedicated service, the servant, thinking that his life and mission was now completed, discovers something astonishing. Entirely surprised, he realizes that God is performing miracles, not only on Abraham's behalf, but also on his behalf. The unobvious becomes the obvious when the servant realizes that God at that moment is thoughtful of him. God has answered the young man's prayer before he has even finished praying. With complete disregard for his surroundings, which includes Rebecca, and all those who traveled with him, the servant comes to what I believe is the apex of the story, the final act. Facedown, the servant worships Abraham's God. In the dust mixed with the mud of the watering hole, the servant, with an overwhelmed heart, publicly worships intimately.

BACKDRAFT

A Worship Story based on Lev 9

THEN Aaron raised his hands towards the people and blessed them. He sacrificed the offering for sin, the burnt offering, and the fellowship offering. Then he came down from the altar. Moses and Aaron went into the tent of meeting. When they came out, they blessed the people. Then, the Lord's glory appeared to all the people. Fire came out from the Lord's presence and consumed the burnt offering, and the pieces of fat on the altar. When all the people saw this, they shouted, and bowed with their faces touching the ground. (Lev 9:24).

The sound came from behind them. Aaron looked back, grabbing Moses by his shoulders, pushing both down hard on the ground. "Look out!"

The heat of the flame passed dangerously close, nearly taking the hair off the back of their necks. Curving like a river bend, the flame directed itself towards the altar and the sacrifice that laid there. In less than an instant, the fat melted away from the sacrifice, leaving the smell of smoke rising to heaven. Amazed, all stood motionless, until someone shouted, then another and then another. Before Moses and Aaron could get to their feet, every father, mother, and child had bowed their faces against the ground. The Lord had come out of the meeting place appearing like a flame; as a backdraft consumed the sweetest part of the sacrifice, on seeing it, the people responded. When the smoke was gone, the smell lingered. It was as if a firestorm had passed, leaving in its wake a smoldering calm. With their faces still on the ground; all were afraid to look. Is it over? Was it safe to get up? Then, one person glanced upward, then another. Soon, everyone was standing again. Their faces turned toward the altar, with no thought of Moses or Aaron. All of them had seen it; it was Jehovah God who had flashed in front of them. Together, they had bowed themselves before the God of the burnt offering.

THOUGHT EXERCISE

Picture this: as you are about to finish your sermon, one that you knew was the best, most powerful word you had ever delivered, suddenly from out of nowhere, without design, there is an unplanned, unexpected change in the middle of the service. In that moment, every word of your presentation that had been so meticulously prepared and so brilliantly delivered instantly dropped out of view. The congregation is awestruck by something other than the prepared service. How would you feel?

If your pulpit ministry were suddenly upstaged by a God visitation with people crying out, falling to the ground, would you issue a complaint to the elders of the church? Would you cry out, "Stop this foolishness"?

Moses and Aaron would not. Behind these highly respected men of ministry, on the altar lay a planned sacrifice of service, so well-planned it was now a tradition that all were overly accustomed to. When a sudden moving of the spirit of God in the form of a winding river of fire surpassed everything that the ministers had offered, the service of sacrifice faded into the background as the people saw God, and together bowed down, worshiping intimately.

Fuming Bees
A Worship Story based on Num 16

Korah, son of Izhar, the son of Kohath, the son of Levi, and certain Reubenites—Dathan and Abiram, sons of Eliah, and son of Peleth became insolent, and rose up against Moses. With them were over 250 Israelite men, well-known community leaders who had been appointed members of the Council. They came as a group to oppose Moses and Aaron, and said to them, "You have gone too far! The whole community is holy, every one of them, and the Lord is with them. Why then do you set yourselves above the Lord's assembly?" When Moses heard this, he fell facedown. (Num 16:1–4).

Bad news travels fast. Before the crowd of offended brothers had found Moses, he had a sense of what was coming, and he prepared himself. Moses was not an easy pushover. He had seen everything that a man could possibly see, and now the 250 frustrated, angry Israelites swarming like fuming bees carried no sting. As their leader assaulted him with practiced words and intimidating threats, the hostility passed through Moses like plasma projected from the sun as the word "holy" burned deep in his spirit. The man was attacking God's holiness, not his own. Then, the significant part revealed itself: "Why do you set yourself above the Lord's assembly?"

If the words had been directed at Joshua, a battle would have come about right there, in that very spot. However, it was Moses, and he was more than a professional warrior—he was an intimate worshiper.

THOUGHT EXERCISE

When faced with a personal challenge, where do we go to find our defense? Some call a brother or sister for advice. Others turn to a trustworthy friend who has experience with such matters. I have known a few people who fight fire with fire, and muscle with muscle. To most, anger is the first response, leading to angry words and violent threats of retaliation. I do not suggest that. Yet, what if the battle that we are facing is beyond our earthly battleground? A spiritual attack of some sort? What then? Paul says to the Ephesians, we never wrestle with flesh and blood, never! All things that come against us are spiritual. Moses did not have the chance to read The Book of Ephesians, but he knew the principle of spiritual warfare.

How do we resist the devil when he brings a swarm of fuming bees to harass us? Some say read God's word and apply the nouns and adjectives and the phrases written in scripture. Others say to conquer evil by doing good. I agree with both; but first, like Moses, I would throw myself to the ground worshiping intimately, allowing God to bring his own personal solution. Bowing facedown before the Lord of heaven's armies brings results.

Worshiping God's Way
A Worship Story based on Deut 5

"You shall not make for yourselves an image in the form of anything in heaven above or on the earth beneath or in the waters below. You shall not bow down to them or worship them; for I, the Lord your God, am a jealous God, punishing the children for the sin of the parents to the third and fourth generation of those who hate me, but showing love to 1,000 generations of those who love me and keep my commandments." (Deut 5:8–10).

    The multitude of survivors stood silently, their gaze fixed on his face, their ears strictly attentive to the words. Within the captivated crowd, young children impatiently turned and twisted as mother's hands squeezed tightly around little fingers to keep them from escaping. In the not-so-far distance, cattle and sheep, goats and camels made their noises. It was a normal day for them, but not for those God followers. Hovering over the vast crowd was a spirit of emergency. This was not just one of those important meetings. The parting of the sea, the food from heaven, the cloud and fire were not as desperate as this final hour. The words read at this moment would mean life or final death for those who would not receive. There was a list, and at the top of the list: true, unadulterated worship. God's jealousy and the punishment that could follow, attached to the promise of love, was intertwined with real heaven-designed worship. At that moment in time, God made it clear there would be no substitutes. For those listening that day, worshiping God's way was rooted deeply in each person's being.

Bowing before God with love, kissing his hands and feet, was a living truth in their world. To those wilderness survivors, worship was bowing with intimacy; they just had to make the choice to do it.

THOUGHT EXERCISE

Looking at the history of mankind, one must wonder: at what instant did bowing before God becomes so important?

The very second the heavens were created, bowing down before the creator was customary worship. It was that simple. From that specific moment in history, the design of worship found its importance. God, at the expense of the universe, premeditated worship for himself.

Have you ever looked at the history of mankind and wondered, at what moment did worship become everything that a man does? Now, that is not so simple, and in reality, it makes no sense. Worshiping God's way has been lost in translation. Now it is only in their hearts that people think they are bowing. Yet, in the beginning, that is not what God professed.

There is coming a day when the multitude of world survivors will, for an instant, stand silently together, gazing towards the sound that is coming from heaven. At that moment, descending before them will be the one who wrote the whole book. When that takes place, there will be no need for mothers to fight with their children as they try to keep them immobile for just a few minutes while a pastor completes his sermon. Cellphones will ring, computers will talk, televisions, cars and planes will continue working, but no one will be paying any attention. Every ear will hear only one thing, and then every knee will bow down and worship, just as God said in the beginning. Read Rom 11. Many will fall on their faces out of fear, others will bow down on their faces with a sigh of relief. Bowing intimately, they will shout, "He is here!"

The Warrior Versus the Commander

A Worship Story based on Josh 5

When Joshua was near Jericho, he looked up and saw a man standing in front of him with a sword in his hand. Joshua went up to him and asked, "Are you one of us or one of our enemies?"

"Neither," he answered. "I am here because I am the commander of the Lord's army."

Joshua fell to his knees and bowed down to the ground. "I am your servant," he said. "Tell me what to do."

"Take off your sandals," the commander answered. "This is a holy place."

So, Joshua took off his sandals. (Josh 5:13–15).

In the distance was the battleground. It was a no man's land with fortified walls that, if there was to be a victory, needed to come down. In full confidence, war was his specialty. Joshua could fight—that was one of his callings. Fixed on the task ahead, the cost was worth the cause, and he was eager to begin. But first, there would be an unexpected meeting. The sword glimmered in the light of the moon as it twisted in the man's hand. His shadow was daunting, while his face was unclear, covered in blackness. Broad shoulders, thick legs and arms that could hold more than his own weight, he had to be more than a common warrior, more than one in the infantry.

The Warrior Versus the Commander

Stepping closer, Joshua's muscles tightened, his forearms and hands gripped the top of his sword, firmly, prepared for what would come next. Without breaking his stride, Captain Joshua drew his line; walking towards the shadow, he would not deviate his course. Stepping aside was not in Joshua's nature. He questioned the statue as his voice deepened. The wrong answer would bring conflict—Joshua was ready. The correct reply would lead to acknowledging leadership with honor.

The shadow replied.

What kind of answer is that? Joshua relaxed his hold. Abruptly, Joshua stopped his pursuit. *This is no mere soldier*, he thought. *His voice, his stance, it is not ordinary.* With an intense stare, his eyes straining to see more than just a figure of the tall forceful voice, Joshua hears the unexpected. "I am the commander of the Lord's army." Joshua says nothing, has no orders to delegate. He does what he has been trained to do: he submits to his authority, the higher chain of command, the final commander. Taking off his battle shoes, Joshua surrenders, his face on the ground.

THOUGHT EXERCISE

Full of human strength and confidence, looking for a place to perform their cause, forcefully taking the ground for the kingdom; that is how many new believers begin their relationship with Jesus. Whatever they see appears as a battleground, with battlements and field strategies that only the brave can implement. So, they enter their Christian service, taking many into the field of battle with them. Certainly, none of us are exempt from this type encounter. All face the battlegrounds found in life. Unfortunately, they come with our first step as a child, a first day at school, from the neighbor who for some reason just does not like us, no matter how hard we tried to be friendly. These, and more, are the walls of Jericho that each will face, and more than once in his or her lifetime. The truth is, there are more of us who would rather avoid the battles, finding our glory elsewhere, and there is nothing wrong with that; God would prefer it. The lesson is, God wants us to see him like Joshua saw him at a moment when the unavoidable, unenjoyable task is in front of us. For both, those who delight in the battle and those who cower at the thought of it, need to see the sword in his hand and hear the words coming out of his mouth. "I am here because . . . I am the commander." He has reason, purpose, and the authority to be there, and we have but one response: to bow our face to the ground. As we worship, the battle is no longer in our mind; the strategies of war are forgotten. Even our battle shoes come off prior to worshiping the commander in chief. So how can you fight without shoes? Unlike prayer, in worship there is no battle, no strategy greater than laying at the feet of the commander, and no act more powerful than intimate worship.

SEVEN MIRACLES
A Worship Story based on Judg 7

AND it was so, when Gideon heard the telling of the dream, and the interpretation thereof, that he worshiped, and returned into the host of Israel, and said, arise; for the Lord hath delivered into your hand the host of the Midian. (Judg 7:15).

In this book, the angel of the Lord, the Lord himself comes to rest beneath a tree as Gideon, unaware of what is about to happen, works below in the wine press. Gideon's journey begins because the people of God have forgotten what true worship was about. Gideon's life challenges are due to faulty worship practices and as the story unfolds, even Gideon demonstrates his lack of worship experience. After seven encounters with the God of Israel, on the seventh time, Gideon, now standing in the enemy's camp, hears the prophetic word, and falling face down, worships God, God's way.

THOUGHT EXERCISE

When is it a good time to do what Gideon did? Is there one? Would we fall facedown if an angel of the Lord showed himself to us, burned a sacrifice in front of us, gave us direct orders, protected us from an angry mob, or poured water on a dry sheep skin? Or would we wait until we were standing before the entrance to the enemy's camp? When a man finds himself completely unmatched

Part Two: Stories of Worship

by the overwhelming measures of his creator, that is when he will bow his face to the ground worshiping the God of prophecy.

Yet, how often does that happen? Speechless, powerless, and caught off guard, that is when a human being will offer sincere worship, regardless of their surroundings. No discussion, bargaining or sharing strategies under the guise of manipulating conversations will bring about intimate worship. Running off to find an expensive gift for the exchange of gratitude will build nothing but frustration, postponing the inevitable. God wants every warrior facedown before the battle begins, and after the battle is over. Intimate worship is the victory.

A Strange Sight
A Worship Story based on Judg 13

So, Manoah took a young goat and a grain offering and sacrificed them to the Lord on a rock he used as an altar. While Manoah and his wife watched, the Lord did something miraculous. As the flame went up toward heaven from the altar, the messenger of the Lord went up in the flame. When Manoah and his wife saw this, they immediately bowed down with their faces touching the ground. (Judg 13:19-20).

Reaching over, he covered her eyes while looking on in horror. The man who had talked with them, who had befriended them, was engulfed in flames before their eyes, somehow sucked into its burning upward path. Bending and turning, he looked contorted, as if melting and stretching like a wax doll. As the flames grew higher, the figure of the man grew with it; it was unimaginable. Pushing his hands from her face, she too viewed with amazement the never-before-seen demonstration of God's power. The flame, glowing red and white, passed through his now-transparent body mixed with orange and black embers, circling him like fireflies. It was a sight that no human eye had ever seen. Who could think of such a thing? The man could have just walked away, disappearing into the night—why a burning fire that appeared to be rising to heaven? Together they watched, then without words, together they bowed themselves on the ground, worshiping God. They had witnessed a miraculously strange sight.

Part Two: Stories of Worship

THOUGHT EXERCISE

With all that we see in the media today, what could bring us to a place of awe? Deep space adventures, superhuman strength, defying gravity, and all human potential; everything is possible on the screen. Today, seeing a man move like an insect climbing up the wall is common practice, as normal as a human being flying like a fireball of flame. All that is imaginable is now believable and easily created for our viewing entertainment.

So, what would it take for us to fall on our knees and worship Jesus? What could amaze us to the point of touching our face to the ground? How about a man who was at one moment standing next to you, then instantly rising towards heaven in a flame of sacrifice? Would that do it? What about the thought of our Lord and Savior, Jesus ascending from a mount into heaven, as men and women stood watching? Would that do it? If not that, then what about the day he returns in the clouds, the same way that he left? You know what the Bible says: "Every knee will bow, and every tongue will confess that Jesus is Lord." (Rom 11). I think that will do it.

The Master of the Harvest

A Worship Story based on Ruth 2

"Ruth immediately bowed down to the ground and said to him, why are you so helpful? Why are you paying attention to me? I am only a foreigner." (Ruth 2:10).

He picked me out of a crowd of people—all of us doing the same thing, working in the same fashion under the heat of the open sun. I did nothing to get his attention, yet he noticed me. Why was that? Looking at him, I knew that I was not like him. *I am from a different place*, I thought to myself as he approached. I am a foreigner, but that did not matter, he still reached out to me. Then, as if someone had thrown a stone, hitting me in the chest, his kindness struck me dead center. I staggered in my mind, hoping he did not notice, but it was too late—he looked right through me. Nonetheless, it was a noble thing, the virtuous look that I saw in him. Nothing like those working around me, who would have done me harm. Somewhere deep inside, I felt his concern for me; it was like the floodwaters filling up an empty well. I warmly bowed before him. If or when I see him again, I would bow again without hesitation.

Part Two: Stories of Worship

THOUGHT EXERCISE

When the master of the harvest comes to us in the heat of the day, and we hear his voice, drinking the water of his words, soaking in his acknowledgment and blessing, how do we respond? Some of us continue working in the field, solely focused on the task of gathering the harvest. Others pause briefly as they contemplate the beneficial rewards that come with serving the master of the field. Even when the master of the field approaches the one harvesting the crop, they often fail to take the time to look up, giving the harvest maker his honor. Like Ruth, perhaps it is best when our place is at the rear, behind those who get the first choice of the harvest: the barley and wheat that is easiest to pick, tasting the best when dried. Most of us do not like the feeling of being behind or in last place, but sometimes that is how things go. I do not think Ruth enjoyed being the one looked down on and mistreated in the workplace, but she worked hard anyway, without complaint. Interestingly, though, she had no problem falling on her face with warmth toward the master of the harvest. I did not see anyone else doing that in the story, did you? True humility produces true worship.

A True Worshiper
A Worship Story based on 1 Sam 1

YEAR after year, this man went from his town to worship and sacrifice to the Lord Almighty at Shiloh, where Hophini and Phinehas, the two sons of Eli, were priests of the Lord. (1 Sam 1:3).

Every year, for many years, he took both of his wives to a worship service that was full of hidden exploitation. He himself had private issues between his two wives, for there was little harmony in his own home. He loved both women but was partial to one. Yet, he religiously came, bowing himself before God in worship and presenting his sacrifice as a service to God. Elkanah, the man with two wives, was a product of a dishonored temple, a place where men refused to take God seriously. The spirit of the times led people to be hard of hearing, lacking God consciousness. It was a dull place. Yet, they all bowed religiously at the altar in Shiloh. Seeing through the haze of secret sin, God spied a true worshiper, one whose heart, mind, soul, and strength accompanied her. Hannah had a reason to bow, and for many years, carrying her burdens silently, unknowing if or when God would answer, she worshiped intimately.

THOUGHT EXERCISE

Are you an Elkanah: a product of a spiritually dead society, governed by sour times? Are you like the second wife, arrogant and insensitive to the wounded feelings of a family member? Are you an Eli, old in service, unable to detect the spiritual climate of your ministry, yet comfortable in the office? Are you one of the two sons of Eli, defiling secretly the worship place of God, justifying your actions by tainted satisfactions? Have you been all the above?

On the other hand, are you like Hannah, who, despite her circumstances, bows before God with her whole being, intimately worshiping in the middle of the perverse community of believers? If that question makes you angry, you need to find a place alone and worship God, seeking a solution. Like Hannah, answers come to transparent worshipers.

THE COST
A Worship Story based on 2 Sam 12

THEN David got up off the ground, washed himself, put on lotions, and changed his clothes. He went to the tabernacle and worshiped the Lord. (2 Sam 12:20).

It had been many days in mourning, and his bad choices had taken its toll. Weakened to the point of collapse, dirty and smelly, he laid there on the floor, a broken commander, leader, and king. Fearing the worst, but petitioning God for favor, he had no idea of what was coming. Nonetheless, he knew he had made a huge mistake. With the verdict announced and the penalty paid, he rose up like a man who had accepted the terms with honor and dignity. However, more than the personal lessons of life, David stood up with a new reality, a fresh taste of where he would lay himself down again. This time, he bowed his face to the ground, not with deep petitions or tearful requests for forgiveness, but with unfathomable sincerity, and true respect. Deep worship is costly.

THOUGHT EXERCISE

To many people, God has a candy-coated shell. If the taste in our mouth is not sweet, we disregard it as not being God. When something pleasing comes to us, we assume it is God's favorable reward, when in many instances it is not. So, how does the word of correction come? Does it float through the door, lingering as sweet perfume, bringing pleasant thoughts to all who smell it? Is his kindness always sympathetic, leading to repentance? If that is true, could the death of David's son have been God's kindness? Lastly, what crucified God's only son? Was it not loving kindness? Interestingly, David said, "I will not offer anything to the Lord that does not cost me something." Bowing before God will cost all of us a portion of something, and it is not always sweet to the taste. If you have not bowed before him, you might want to do it before he kindly reminds you of the cost that his son paid so we could find the meaning of worship.

Troubled Times
A Worship Story based on 1 Kgs 1

Solomon is now seated on the royal throne. Furthermore, the royal officials have come to congratulate his Majesty, King David, saying, "May your God make Solomon's name more famous than yours and his reign greater than your reign." The King himself bowed down on his bed and said, "Praise the Lord God of Israel, who has let me see the heir to my throne." (1 Kgs 1:46–48).

It is, again, troubled times. David, even in his last days as King, due to broken family relationships, faces opposition. His own blood is strategizing against one another to secure a place at the king's table. Nearly bedridden, struggling to stay warm, his frail body cannot carry him, but his mind is sharp. When the news reaches him, the plan is instant and final. *Solomon will take my place; he will be king.*

Solomon, pronounced king, returns to the city of David. The processional as loud as thunder shakes the ground as the crowd escorts him into his place of kingship, but his father is not there to see. High above the streets, in a dark room, lying on his bed, David shivers uncontrollably; his bones are extremely cold. Hearing that all has gone as planned, he removes the heavy blankets from his chest and painfully lifts himself to an upright position. With help from his servant, he pulls himself even further forward, sliding his knees beneath his chest. After forty years of worshiping in the city that carried his name, David bows on his bed and worships intimately. It will be his last time.

Part Two: Stories of Worship

THOUGHT EXERCISE

The broken family is an age-old problem. Spoiled children, parents who fail to set boundaries and discipline their children, even going as far as never saying a harsh word to their unruly offspring, is not a new thing. Rather, it has been a common practice throughout the centuries. If you read this story about David, he never questioned his son Adonijah, never! That tells us something right there—troubled times are ahead. For the record, it is not always the parents' fault. Kids are people, too; born with a sinful nature, some are worse than others, some better. So, if you do have trouble with your children, do not blame it all on yourself, unless you failed to talk to them; and even then, there are no guarantees.

Then, there is the suffering. It hurts when our children go through a dark time, becoming rebellious, setting out on their own, heading for what a parent sees as something destructive. I think it is that feeling of losing control of the situation that is the worst. Like when we would tell them to look both ways before crossing the street, or not to touch that, it's hot. Losing that authority brings panic.

Laying on his bed, the man after God's own heart could do nothing but wait and hope for the best. One son would suffer; the other would obtain the highest honor. I think David would have wanted both children to succeed. Bedridden, David's last act was to thankfully bow before his God. That, too, was a lesson that David wanted both of his sons to learn. By the way, when was the last time you spoke to your children about the way they were acting? When was the last time you spoke to them about bowing before God, worshiping him intimately? Both are important.

The History of Worship
A Worship Story based on 2 Kgs 17

When you read 2 Kgs 17: 7-34, the word worship is the word for fear and service, not bowing down, which you can find in some translations. In 2 Kgs 17:35-39, the word for worship is bowing down.

"The disaster came upon the people of Israel because they feared other gods. (2 Kgs 7:1). Yes, they feared idols. Despite the Lord's specific and repeated warning. (2 Kgs 7:12). They feared worthless idols, so they became worthless themselves. (2 Kgs 7:15). They did not turn from these sins until the Lord finally swept them away from his presence. (2 Kgs 7:18). But since these foreign settlers did not worship, bowing down before the Lord when they first arrived, the Lord sent lions among them, which killed some of them. (2 Kgs 7:25). They sent one of the exiled priests back to Samaria. Let him live here and teach the new residents the religious customs of the God of the land." (2 Kgs 17:27).

"And though they worshiped the Lord, they continue to follow their own gods. (2 Kgs 7:29). According to the religious customs of the nations from which they came. They continue to follow their former practices. Instead of truly worshiping the Lord. (2 Kgs 7:33). For the Lord had made a covenant with the people . . . Do not bow before any other God. You must worship only the Lord your God, He is the one who will rescue you from all your enemies. But the people would not listen . . . they worship the Lord, and their idols." (2 Kgs 17:35- 40).

Part Two: Stories of Worship

The people invited to live on God's land offended him by not fearing him. Because of this, God removed his presence from them. With the people removed, another group of people settled in the land that once belonged to them. This new assembly of people had no idea how to fear God, God's way, but God gave them a chance to learn. God sent a man to explain what fearing God is, and they comprehended it; however, they were unwilling to give up their customary religious ideas.

God clearly presented his commandments to this new generation who were non-Israelites, having a history of idol worship, but it did not sink in. History repeated itself as the people failed to worship God in the way that pleased Him. As time passed, God continued to look for another group of people who would worship him intimately. He went back to the first group again, but again, they failed to see it. This is the history of worship.

THOUGHT EXERCISE

When Jesus met the woman of Samaria at the well, people were still discussing the history of worship. Which group of people had worshiped correctly was the topic of the day. The Samaritans accused the Hebrews, and the Hebrews disagreed with the Samaritans. Both have sinned against God, while neither of them worship God in a way that pleased him. They all had secret agendas and religious customs they would not give up. Thus, the most powerful place on earth, which is his presence, was swept away again, like a river evaporating in a desert. Jesus says, in The Book of John chapter 4 verse 24, that God is looking for people who will bow intimately, and that those who call themselves worshipers will, in reality, actually worship. Like history, the search for worshipers continues. Do you see it? Are you ready to be a worshiper?

The Bystander, Part One
A Worship Story based on 1 Chron 29

AND David said to all the congregation, "Now, bless the Lord your God." And all the congregation, blessed the Lord God of their fathers, and bowed down their heads, and worshiped the Lord, and the king. (1 Chron 29:20).

I stood there with all of them, listening. "He has been a good king," I said to the man standing next to me. He fought our battles, protected us with his own blood, but he was not perfect, of course. Nonetheless, honest with a Godlike heart, I always liked listening to him. He was transparent, with nothing to prove, nothing to defend—just sharing his life with us. Never was he timid, or embarrassed to show his love for his God, and that counted. In the streets or in the temple, he was always the same man—David, son of Jesse.

Now, it is his son's time. Solomon. Yes, God has been our blessing, I agree with that, and hopefully his son will be as wise; but experienced, perhaps not? David is right. God has chosen his son to finish the job. I am so glad it is not me. I like it out here in the crowd, where there is no pressure to perform, and no rules other than to worship God and serve him only. I can do that.

King David's prayer was long. I think that comes with old age. I do not mind that, either. It was a good meeting, powerful, and at the end, we all bowed our heads. All of us like following the instructions of our King David.

The Bystander, Part Two
A Worship Story based on 2 Chron 7

Now, when Solomon had made an end of praying, fire came down from heaven, and consumed the burnt offering, and the sacrifices; and the glory of the Lord filled the house. And the priests could not enter the house of the Lord because the glory of the Lord had filled the Lord's house. And when all the children of Israel saw how the fire came down, and the glory of the Lord upon the house, they bowed themselves with their faces to the ground upon the pavement, and worshiped, and praise the Lord, saying, "For he is good; for his mercy endures forever." (2 Chron 7:1-7).

I was there too, right in the heart of it. A prayer, and that was it. No one had to tell us what to do next. There was fire, offerings, smoke filling every inch of the room. The ministers could not even get in. I found myself facedown. Somehow, we began singing over and over again, "He is good, his mercy endures forever!"

THOUGHT EXERCISE

David prayed a long prayer, then said, "Now let us all bow our heads." His son offered a short prayer and gave no instruction as God's presence filled the room. Being told to do something is one thing, while just doing it is another thing. Obedience shows respect, while spontaneous, heart-felt response leads to intimate

The Bystander, Part Two

worship. Will the smoke come again—should it have to? His mercy still endures.

The Answer
A Worship Story based on 2 Chron 20

FRIGHTENED, Jehoshaphat decided to ask for the Lord's help. He announced a fast throughout Judah. The people of Judah gathered to see the Lord's help. They came from every city in Judah.... Then the Lord's Spirit came to Jahaziel (descendant of Asaph). He said, "Pay attention to me, everyone from Judah, everyone living in Jerusalem, and King Jehoshaphat. This is what the Lord says to you: do not be frightened or terrified by this large crowd. The battle it is not yours. It is God's. Tomorrow go into battle against them. They will be coming up Ziz pass. You will find them at the end of the valley in front of the Jeruel desert. You will not fight this battle. Instead, just take your position, stand still, and see the victory of the Lord for you, Judah and Jerusalem. Do not be frightened or terrified. Tomorrow go out to feast. The Lord is with you. Jehoshaphat bowed down with his face touching the ground. Everyone from Judah and the people who lived in Jerusalem immediately bowed down in front of the Lord. The Levites, descendants of Kohath and Korah, stood up to praise the Lord, God of Israel with very loud songs. (2 Chron 20:3-4, 15-19).

"They are here!" his servant announced.

"All of them?" he asked.

"Yes, every tribe is waiting."

Over the last several days, he had worried over what he thought would be his demise. He was not a bad king, at least not as bad as some, but the idea had run through his mind. *What could I*

The Answer

have done to avoid this? The thought of being beheaded in front of all Israel was enough to cause any grown man fear, so much—but seeking God could be the only solution.

In front of him stood every person in every tribe. They too were afraid, fearful of losing their husbands and wives, children and grandchildren, their homes, and the land that had come to them by way of the promise. With their eyes full of desperation, they stared at him, looking for something that would give them a glimmer of hope, but there was nothing. Their king, the leader of all Jewish people, had come to this end. He pronounced publicly that he was done. The king had no plans, not even a way to escape. His only plea: seek God! Awkwardly, this tiny nation became a large gathering of God-seekers. In the past, the answer had come as a fire, and the cloud, some looked up thinking it would come like manna. What were they waiting for? How would the answer come this time?

At a moment when the silence became weighted, from the front of the meeting place a small voice rang out. "Pay attention to me," it said. Only the few standing near the front could see who it was; the rest could only be still as they made themselves focus on the little voice coming from somewhere in the massive crowd. Unusual, no one questioned the words they all knew it was the answer. Unlike the power that came with the flood, forcing Noah's boat off dry land, this answer like a mist drifted over the heads and into their ears. Entering their hearts, the words of truth brought the people and their fearful leader to a place they did not know existed until that moment. The answer had come in a way that was unexpected, unplanned, and without the possibility of rehearsal. This was itself part of the miracle. A young musician, whose great, great, and even greater grandfather was Asaph, had the answer in him; it was the gift of prophecy. The God of the fearful king used this young man's gift to speak out the directions that led to a successful strategy. Grasping his heart, the king had only one response. In full view of his kingdom, he placed himself face down on the ground and worshiped intimately as the nation of God-seekers followed.

87

PART TWO: STORIES OF WORSHIP

THOUGHT EXERCISE

This is an even shorter version. There was an important man who had a serious question, so he called a meeting. The prophetic word came from the unexpected, and the people who were listening received it in their hearts, believing it was the answer. Then, the same man bowed on the ground. (I guess you could say he took the role of the worship leader.) The gathering followed, and together they had an intimate time of worship. The praise service came later. For reference, read 1 Cor 14:24–25; you will see some similarities.

The Grand Opening
A Worship Story based on 2 Chron 29

He had the Levites stand in the Lord's Temple with symbols, hearts, and lyres as David, the King's searing seer Gad, and the prophet Nathan had ordered. This command came from the Lord through his prophets. The Levites stood with David's instruments, and the priests had the trumpets. Then Hezekiah ordered the sacrificing of burnt offerings on the altar. When the burnt offerings started, the song of the Lord started. These songs were accompanied by trumpets and the instruments of King David of Israel. The whole assembly bowed down, with their faces touching the ground. Singers began to sing, and the trumpets blew until the burnt offering was finished. When the burnt offerings were finished, the King, and everyone who was with him, kneeled, and bowed down. Then King Hezekiah and the leaders called the Levites to praise the Lord with the words of David and the seer Asaph. They joyfully sang praises, bowed down and worshiped. (2 Chron 29:25-29).

"We are going to do it just like the book said," the young king insisted. "All of you know, God told David, through the prophets, exactly what he wanted. Cymbals, harps, stringed instruments, and even the old ones on the trumpets to, we will do it his way, not our own." It had been years since anyone had stepped inside the worship place, and all had forgotten what it looks like. Every inch needed cleaning. Bowls, knives, and forks. The table and the steps leading to the altar, the handles on the doors and the tall-draped walls had to be cleaned. In a total of sixteen days, it was completed.

Part Two: Stories of Worship

For the grand opening, the doors opened wide. The order of service was simple: bring the bulls to the altar; as the sacrifice begins, the king nods his head, and the songs begin, except this song was no ordinary, or modern-day folk tune—it was the "Song of the Lord." The Lord's song, a song that the Lord himself would occupy. Not found in the instruction of service, nor planned in the itinerary, the guests freely in their own manner, responded to the Lord's song. One after the other, they bowed themselves on the ground, worshiping together. Looking out over the crowd, seeing the top of their heads, the king realized what had happened. The Lord was claiming his song, and all flesh within the sound of his voice was humbled by his presence. Not really knowing what to do next, the young man ordered the musicians to play the old songs, the songs that some had forgotten, a song from the past king. The praise rose, and again God's presence superseded the order of service, and everyone, including the leader King, bowed intimately on the ground.

THOUGHT EXERCISE

Over time, church buildings get old, needing updating and deep cleaning. Carpets get dusty, the seats smell of old perfume and moth-eaten tweed suit jackets. Despite parent's orders, kids stick gum under the pews, which is hard to get off. Instead of cleaning up an old building, for some it would be easier to just move to a new place or build something modern and up to date. We buy plastic-wrapped chairs with no stains, a new soundboard with automated faders, big speakers, and bright monitors to fill the stage with sound, and this is just the start of it. The list is endless. We cannot forget the screens, projectors, computers, and stage lights. When all is in place, it smells fresh, looking shiny like a new car, but the truth is, all of that will wear off, and not soon after will need thorough cleaning and updating.

In 2 Chronicles, the leader/pastor/king is twenty-five years old, and he is the symbol of a new generation. What is cool about this young man is instead of trying to be at the cutting edge of his generation, the Lord reminds him of the past, a time long before his own parents' or grandparents' time. The Lord leads this young man to discover something so old, it was new. With conviction and authority, he accepts the challenge and makes a declaration. "This place of worship has been abandoned, so we are cleaning this mess up, not according to our new way of worshiping, but according to God's prophetic word to my great-great-grandfather David."

The lesson in this chapter is this: to do something God's way, you first need a revelation of what his word says. Then, you need the guts to follow through with his instructions. This is no easy task, especially when it affects how people worship. Sometimes intimate worship needs cleaning up.

Contagious Worship
A Worship Story based on Ezra 9 and 10

At that time of the sacrifice, I stood up from where I had sat in the morning with my clothes torn. I fell to my knees and lifted my hands to the Lord my God. I prayed. (Ezra 9:5).

While Ezra prayed and made this confession, weeping and lying face down on the ground in front of the temple of God, a large crowd of people from Israel, men, women and children—gathered and wept bitterly with him. (Ezra 10:1).

Praise overflowing and with great expectations, Ezra led a host of captives to a place that was to be their second promise land. So important was the return of the captive ones that each person's name was written down on a list of names. If your name was there, you were special. Not too soon after his arrival, grief replaced his praise, and the hope for the return of God's presence faded. "Oh my God, I am utterly ashamed," Ezra cries out to God. The words brought him to his knees; he bows himself facedown with little room between his face and the dirt. Ezra had become a desperate worshiper. Yet, in weakness, his hands extended upward in praise, as he pleads again for deliverance. The circumstances of life, which led Ezra to mourning and tears, produced intimate worship. Without public invitation, the nation of Israel joined him—intimate worship is contagious.

THOUGHT EXERCISE

What is the ingredient that makes a person a true worshiper? I can tell you that desperation plays a huge part. Desperate times lead to desperate measures, and bowing down outside the temple in the dirt was nothing short of complete desperation. Ezra's encounter with an unsatisfied God produced widespread desperation. The sense that God was unhappy about the people's relationship with him was not only within Ezra; those who lived in the community felt it, too.

Can you remember the last time someone said God was unsatisfied about something? Does anyone do that anymore? Has God stopped revealing his feelings about the things people do? God's word is so full of things that he is unsatisfied with—do we know what those things are? I have heard more sermons on prosperity, attaining your destiny, walking in Christ's blessings—enough to satisfy me for the next fifty years. Yet, when I look, very few people are desperate for the things of God. We need a move of spiritual desperation. When I see people bowing face down, worshiping intimately outside the church building, I will know the time of desperation has come.

True Revival
A Worship Story based on Neh 8

EZRA the scribe stood on a high wooden platform that had been made for the occasion.... Ezra, standing higher than all the other people, opened the book in front of them. As he opened it, all the people stood to their feet. Ezra thanked the Lord, the great God. All the people responded, "Amen! Amen!" As they raised their hands, they then bowed with their faces to the ground and worshiped the Lord.... "Don't mourn or weep on such a day is this! For today is a sacred day before the Lord your God." For the people had all been weeping as they listened to the words of the law. (Neh 8:4–6, 9).

"Just put it right there, in the middle," he said, pointing. "I am not that tall, but I think everyone should be able to see me from here." With one foot and then the next, Ezra tested it out. The box was sturdy. He would be heads above everyone, and that would work.

"Make sure you talk loud enough; some of the old ones cannot hear too good," a helper suggested. Out in the open, everyone who was old enough to understand gathered, most of whom sat on the ground waiting for the service to begin. It was an outdoor meeting, the first of its kind in over one hundred years. A true revival meeting.

Standing on the box, he cleared his throat as he carefully opened the book. Delicately, he tried to not to tear the pages, for the book was worth far beyond any amount one could pay. The first page turned. Those who were sitting in the hot sun stood to their

TRUE REVIVAL

feet, silently waiting to hear the short man's words. With his hands raised to heaven, the reader gave his "YADA" (Hebrew for lifting hands in praise) to the Lord. Those who watched shouted confirmation with a loud amen as they offered their praise, stretching their hands towards the heavens of Jehovah. One, then another; soon, all were bowed facedown before the power of the book and the greatness of its true author.

Before the reading of the word was complete, the living truth found in the book filled the people's hearts and minds, and all of them, facedown, worshiped God intimately. Moments later came the reading of the words, and their tears flowed like a river of revival.

THOUGHT EXERCISE

Maybe it is just me, but I do not get it. Why is it that every time the pastor stands behind the pulpit, raising his hands towards heaven or opening the book, people think it is time to sit down? Am I missing something? Let us not talk about worshiping—I would not mind seeing a few tears, but that does not happen, either. Clearly, there needs to be the revival of intimate worship.

An Age-Old Problem
A Worship Story based on Esth 3

"When Haman saw that Mordecai would not bow down or show him respect, he was filled with rage." (Esth 3:5).

Her uncle's only concern was for her safety. Mordecai was not looking for promotion through his adopted daughter's good fortune; what he did find was God's plan for a nation of God worshipers.

"Why isn't he bowing before me?" Haman shouted.

"He is a Jew," his servant replied with fear.

"Jew or not, he will bow!"

Mordecai refused. "I will not bow before any god or man. I only worship Jehovah."

The stage was set. The challenge was coming, and only God knew the outcome. Knowing something was in the air, Mordecai stood firm at his post. This was no longer about Esther; it had become something of far greater importance. It was about a captive people who at one time understood intimate worship, but by now had lost sight of what it meant to be a worshiping nation.

THOUGHT EXERCISE

This is an age-old problem. The devil wants all of us to worship him. Read what Jesus said in the book of Matthew, Chapter 4. In the book of Esther, we see what Satan really wants. He is not asking for a thought of worship, nor a song, nor a service of some kind, but the actual occurrence of worship. This is what Haman, the devil, was mad about. It is encouraging to see how God took Esther from rags to riches, finding favor with the king and receiving all the blessings. I like that about my father. Equally important is the story of true worship. This, for me, is the underlying back story found in the book of Esther. If threatened impalement by a spear, who would refuse the order to bow down? That itself proves the magnitude and importance of the act of bowing before God in intimate worship. Could it be that the devil is not that angry today, since very few people actually worship God's way? If Mordecai had just politely bowed before his adversary, all his troubles would have vanished. The devil said the same thing to Jesus. If Mordecai had complied, the book of Esther would have had a far different ending. If Jesus had submitted to Satan, the book would not have been written at all. Intimate worship matters.

Too Much Advice
A Worship Story based on Job 31

If I have rejoiced over my great wealth, the fortune my hands had gained, if I had regarded the sun in its radiance or the moon moving in splendor, so that my heart was secretly enticed and my hand offered them a kiss of homage, then these also would be sins to be judged, for I would have been unfaithful to God on high. (Job 31:25–28).

"How many more people are going to give me advice?" Job said, taking a long deep breath, then pouring out the air with a chest-rattling sigh. With his head tilted downward, his eyes nearly closed, he was truly exhausted. All of them were gone; yet, for some reason, he accepted the unexpected events. Poor health consumed him, and that, too, appeared to be behind him now. It was not the money, the livestock, or the lost harvests that mattered. The family reputation no longer existed, nor did his children. In all his injuries, Job never looked up at the heavens, saying, "Oh how wonderful you are." His bank account, as large as it was, did not produce his joy. He did not chuckle when he counted his coins. Job at no time kissed the hands or feet of idols, but faithfully saved his worship for the one true God. Before his life trials, Job was a faithful intimate worshiper. At the end of his life trials, he remained a faithful intimate worshiper.

THOUGHT EXERCISE

Do any of us faithfully bow before God, as if kissing his feet? That is the posterior of true worship. In the New Testament, there were many times when people bowed down before Jesus, kissing his feet. It was priority. When Jesus ascended to heaven, was this precedent of worshiping at his feet discontinued? Did the act of worship disappear or go with him? Has God changed his mind about faithful worship?

Without unexpected trials, our concern for God is rare. We might be anxious about denying the blood of Jesus when talking about the unsaved or neglecting the Holy Spirit when moving in the gifts, or even forgetting to serve him in some manner, but those things are not anxieties based on faithfully bowing with a kiss. If I told you that bowing down before God with love is just as important to him as all the other things we do, would you believe me? Job would. If we care about being faithful to God in small things, how can we be unfaithful in true worship? Rather, let us faithfully kiss his feet in intimate worship before the trials of life, and long after they have passed.

The Transparent Man
A Worship Story based on Ps 138

I bow before your holy Temple as I worship. I praise your name for your unfailing love and faithfulness. For your promises are backed by all the honor of your name. (Ps 138:2).

Everyone in the kingdom had seen the king as a transparent man. Leading the crowd, he danced in the streets, shouting and singing with his hands lifted toward heaven. He commonly played songs with great skill, interpreting in song what his heart was feeling. He laid his life down for his friends, fighting battles from the front lines, protecting the kingdom with his own sword. When his spirit became full of pride and arrogance, and sin led him to a bad place, he took the weight and responsibility on himself, announcing his sins to all who would listen. He was a transparent man. Knowing that everyone was watching, lying down on the ground, like Ezra, before the temple, David intimately worshiped with transparency.

THOUGHT EXERCISE

In the book of Psalms, Chapter 138, there are several things that lead me to believe in the transparent character of David, the psalmist king. He was not shy about expressing himself. Praise in the form of lifting his hands, "Yada," was common when he was around. Songs flowed from his spirit, and he shared them

The Transparent Man

frequently, encouraging others to do the same. Prayer was key to his success, and with honesty, before his creator, he made his request known. His belief that God created him and that he had a future in God's kingdom was his written theology. In all of this, what makes me believe that he was a transparent man was his willingness to bow down before God, in view of his friends and fellow citizens, without the fear of losing his reputation. Intimate worship is transparent.

The Peaceful Solution
A Worship Story based on Prov 28

God detests the prayers of the person who ignores the law (Torah). (Prov 28:9).

"You shall have no other gods before me. You shall not make for yourselves an image in the form of anything in heaven above or on the earth beneath or in the waters below. You shall not bow down to them; for I, the Lord your God, am a jealous God, punishing the children for the sin of the parents to the third and fourth generation of those who hate me, but showing love to a thousand generations of those who love me and keep my commandments." (Deut 5:7–10).

"It's just the first ten Commandments. That is the Books of Law, Moses," the man argued, "not all 622 Commandments, those came later!"

"If you follow one, you have to follow all the others! It is the law!" The other man argued.

"We are not under the law anymore. Jesus did away with that, that is what his death was all about."

The two men debated for over an hour, and neither had gained any ground. Then the solution came, a few feet away at another table. A man sat listening as they spewed verse after verse like fiery darts. Quietly, he got up.

"Excuse me," the man carefully interrupted.

Surprised for a moment, their faces rejected the intrusion, yet they allowed him into their circle.

"I don't mean to interfere with your conversation," the man politely introduced himself. "No. By all means," one of them said reluctantly. Taking a chair, he sat down at their table.

It had only been five minutes or so when he stood, thanking them, and then walked away. The two men sat motionless. It was as if an angel had delivered the good news.

"He is right!" one said to the other.

"Here, but let me buy you some coffee."

"Oh no! Let me."

THOUGHT EXERCISE

The answer is simple. When you find yourself defending a position of faith for God's sake, you first need to ask yourself this question: Does God need my defense? Or is it really for my sake that I argue my case? The Samaritan woman in John 4 knew the law. The people, whom she was angry with, also understood the law. Jesus had come to fulfill the law of God, and he did it perfectly. To know what Jesus knew about the law of his father, read the first two commandments. They are extremely important for a person who wants to be a God worshiper. The first commandment is all about intimate worship.

The Peaceful Solution, Part Two

A Worship Story based on Eccl 12

Now all has been heard; here is the conclusion of the matter: fear God and keep his commandments, for this is the duty of all mankind. (Eccl 12:13).

After they had finished their coffee, the peaceful solution hovered with a twist of fragrant coffee aroma. It was not that hard to figure out, but they both realized they had made it much harder than it was. They were both arguing from a religionist pulpit.

"He was right, if we really fear God and do what his words say, it will be all good."

"No fears—that is the wrong slogan, we need more fear!" The two laughed together.

"And more of his word in our hearts, like that guy said. Bowing down in worship before God is the solution. Where did he go, anyway?"

THOUGHT EXERCISE

The discussion is over; it is time for a conclusion. If you do not understand the fear of God, you will find it hard to worship him. Why is that? Seeing God in his strength comes from encounters that bring a taste of fear. Fear of what he is capable of is a good thing—it builds honest respect. How many of us have honest

The Peaceful Solution, Part Two

respect for God? When we respect someone, we have the tendency to listen to what they say, and hopefully follow their instructions. A product of Godly fear is Godly hearing, which leads to Godly worship. Godly worship is bowing down intimately, with full respect and a faint taste of fear.

Awaken My Love
A Worship Story based on Song

"Promise me, the women of Jerusalem by the gazelles and wild deer, not to awaken love until the time is right . . . .
Promise me, the women of Jerusalem by the gazelles and wild deer, not to awaken love until the time is right . . . .
Promise me, a woman of Jerusalem, not to awaken love until the time is right."
(Song 2:7, 3:5, 8:5).

This was not the first time they had sat on the couch together having this conversation. Tenderly, she tried explaining what it was about and how things worked, but by the look on her face, it was not sinking in.

"It means more when you wait. You cannot just rush into it like that," her mother explained.

"Why does it matter? If I want to do it, why can't I?"

"A lot of people do, and it doesn't seem to bother them, but to others, it does."

With the heart of a mother, she knew that her beloved daughter was trying to process her mother's words, and for someone just turning thirteen, it was not easy.

"Love is hard enough to understand, much less explain. In real time, waiting for it makes it even more difficult, because no one around us wants to do it that way."

"It is not a crime, Mom! I mean, all I want to do is lay my face down on the ground and offer my love to him, why is that so hard to accept?"

Her mother gently replied.

"People accept the fact that bowing before God is real; they just feel uncomfortable about it. You'd be better off if you waited and did it somewhere when the time is right, not on a Sunday morning when everyone is singing."

"Mom, I love God with all my heart. It is like he has awakened my love, and I have to give it back."

Her eyes sparkled with sincerity and her words rose softly like sweet perfume. She was young, but she was old enough to recognize intimate worship.

"Okay, I get it." Her mother agreed. "When you feel the awakening in your heart, you decide when the time is right. I will leave that up to you."

THOUGHT EXERCISE

The words found in the Song of Solomon are more than a text describing an ancient love affair. It is much more than a love story of Solomon and the Queen of Sheba. The writings reveal God's interactive senses. Just like the shared love between a man and a woman, God has feelings that involve expressive response. When he encounters his creation, in that moment of passion, there is a beginning point, and the climax. This true experience is subject to time, and we should know there is no rushing an intimate moment. God does not just perform for his beloved; he waits for the moment to be right, so the two spirits, God's and human's, can equally engage.

Oh, some people say they are not emotional, and that showing their feelings is too embarrassing—politely said, that is hogwash! Every created thing on earth shows some level of emotional response to their creator, and humans have the most to give—and need to receive even a greater portion in return. No human being is lacking in human affections; it is a matter of awakening

PART TWO: STORIES OF WORSHIP

love at the right time. When that takes place, intimate worship is unavoidable.

Kings and Princes
A Worship Story based on Isa

The Lord, the Redeemer, says to the one who is despised and rejected by the nations, to the one who is the servant of rulers, "Kings will stand at attention when you pass by. Princes will also bow low because of the Lord, the faithful one, the holy one of Israel, who has chosen you." (Isa 49:7).

Despised and rejected by all people throughout all time, Jesus still, at this moment, stands as Redeemer. When the time comes, he will pass by all human flesh, and those who were kings of the earth will stand in honor, giving up their prestigious chair in place of praise. Those princes who wore their robes and riches on their shoulders for public display will bow face down in the dirt. As the weight of their sin presses down on them, they will offer themselves not as a prince, but as a worshiper. All of this will happen because the Lord's word is faithful and true. "I seek those who will worship me." John 4:24.

THOUGHT EXERCISE

When the presence of God passes by a human soul, two things can happen. They stand in awe as a form of praise, or they bow low, worshiping intimately. Like the principalities found in heaven's airways who recognize the Lord of creation, humankind, when it encounters its Redeemer, cannot deny the Lordship of Christ.

Part Two: Stories of Worship

When the cornea of the mortal eye catches the reflection of him, the picture is an imprint, like a painted canvas in the mind that visually demands a response. To deny the response is to despise and reject him. The truthful reaction is natural: you stand, or you bow. You praise, or you worship. Have you noticed that nowhere in scripture do you find a person sitting in awe, or resting comfortably in their recliner, as they watch the Lord of heaven casually pass by? If kings can stand and princes can bow low, where do we fit in? If you cannot bow, at least stand. Like the song says, "Christ is worthy of it all."

Scarecrows in a Cucumber Field

A Worship Story based on Jer

WHAT did your ancestors find wrong with me that led them to stray far from me? They worshiped worthless idols, only to become worthless themselves. (Jer 2:5).

Worship at its worst—that is the book of Jeremiah. The generational curse, plaguing family after family, this is the story of worship at its worst. Idolatry leads to adultery, a byproduct of worship at its worst. Yet, when worship is at its worst, there is a message. "A time is coming." In the book of Jeremiah, God calls fishermen and hunters to route the disabled, pulling the wounded with persuasive speech out of their lethargic state. His goal is to catch people before the effects of sin take hold in another generation. When the Lord shows his power, opening the people's hearts to the flood of grace, their despicable acts appear to them like a scarecrow in a cucumber field. (Jer 10:5).

THOUGHT EXERCISE

If we think bowing down before God is only for a past generation of God seekers, we are no better off than those whom we read about in the book of Jeremiah. Rather, we are worse off, for not worshiping God, God's way. For it is idolatry, plain and simple. Yet, we live beneath the covenant of grace, which leads some to

PART TWO: STORIES OF WORSHIP

read only the good parts of God's word: the promises, the mercies, and rewards. Doing this, we limit what we can be and fail to apply to our everyday lives the whole truth. I say that because all of us struggle with stubborn, selfish hearts. So stubborn, we fight against the one thing that God wants, which is a people who will worship him intimately. To think that we could be worthless is contrary to our religious practices. Nonetheless, the Bible says, what we worship is what we become, and no one wants to be a scarecrow in a cucumber field.

Dare to Hope
A Worship Story based on Lam

"Not a King in all the earth, no one in all the world would have believed that an enemy could march through the gates of Jerusalem. Yet, it happened because of the sins of her prophets and the sins of her priests who defiled the city, by shedding innocent blood." (Lam 4:12-13).

"Is there anything I can do?" he asked somberly.

Before she could reply, he knew the answer. With faint breath, she replied, "I never thought this would happen, never in a million years."

There was nothing he could say to her at that moment; no one could have ever guessed how bad things could get. With deep pain, he tried to think of something, even the smallest thing that would change the outcome, but his heart was empty, and so were his words.

"I will never forget this awful time," she said as a line of tears marked her soft skin, and her lips quivered uncontrollably. "This is too great a loss."

Listening in silence, one verse surfaced in his mind. Touching her shoulder, he whispered in his spirit these words. "Yet, I still dare to hope, Lam 3:21. Yet, I still dare to hope."

PART TWO: STORIES OF WORSHIP

THOUGHT EXERCISE

There is a time when worship has no intimacy, no life, and no hope. How can we bow when our heart is broken? For this reason, worship is not mentioned in the book of Lamentations—it was a time of mourning. Every stone in every street, every rock in each wall, and each mortar step that led to each home had been overrun by violent invaders of the soul. Sin had found its way into the life of God's favorite place—the people of his kingdom, and so worship suffered unimaginable loss. Yet, like The Book of Lamentations, the spirit of the broken worshiper secretly holds onto a faint scent of expectation. Out of the depth of the spirit comes a fragrant whisper: "I dare to hope."

When God comes faithfully to lost hope, worship reappears with a great sense of intimacy. This is a word to you: "Don't lose hope!" Like the city of our God, intimate worship will reappear.

A Glimpse of the Future
A Worship Story based on Ezekl

I saw the glory of the God of Israel, coming from the east. His voice was like the sound of rushing water, and the earth was shining because of his glory. This vision was like the one I saw when He came to destroy Jerusalem, and like the one I saw by the Chebar River. I immediately bowed down. The Lord's glory came into the temple through the Eastgate. (Ezek 43:3).

He had seen it all: the north and south gateways, the walls, the courtyards, the rooms for the preparation of the sacrifices in the rooms for the priests. As the vision unfolded, nothing was hidden from his mind's eye. There were many questions, but the prophet had no doubt that God had given him a glimpse into the future. The depth of its meaning would unravel over time, and the true purpose of the dream would in later history fall into place. Yet, however amazing the vision had been, it was not until he saw the glory, heard the voice, and realized the coming devastation that he responded in full force to the apparition. His mind full of God's overwhelming majesty, the prophet had only one reaction to what he had seen. With all that he had in him, he bowed down in intimate worship.

Part Two: Stories of Worship

THOUGHT EXERCISE

Joel 2:28 begins like this: "After this, I will pour my spirit on everyone."

Since the middle of the second century, Christians have clashed with one another over their belief concerning the power of the spirit of God, and the gift of the prophetic. Whether visions, or words containing God's plan, or poignant utterance of encouragement, the lack of interest in the Holy Spirit's gifts wanes with each generation that passes. Strangely, in the midst of rejection, the success of the prophetic voice of God seems to be subject to the one who claims it. Read Corinthians. God's man can refuse the work of the spirit. Regardless of men's poor choices, God is patient and so loving that he allows his children to choose how they utilize the most powerful portion of his personality—the most Holy Spirit.

How could God force a word or a vision on someone? Even Ezekiel welcomed God's gifts. Before practicing a theological discourse of the pros and cons of the gifts of the Holy Spirit, my suggestion to you is to invite as much of the Holy Spirit's intervention into your life as you possibly can. That way, when the world tries to convince you that the prophetic purposes of God were for a past generation, you will not believe such a teaching. Let's be honest— what better way to lead someone into a place of intimate worship than by explaining a vision or a dream, or giving a personal word of encouragement that reveals the secrets of their own heart? That is how Paul said to do it. (Cor 14). The prophetic voice leads to intimate worship.

THE LAST SONG
A Worship Story based on Dan 3

"I will give you one more chance to bow down and worship the statue I have made, when you hear the sound of the musical instruments." (Dan 3:15).

With or without the music, the three men did not intend on obeying the king's orders. It would not happen. They would die before bowing before a wooden statue surrounded by false praise. The music played loudly as the people offered foreign sounds to a foreign god, and when the music found its climax, it suddenly ended on cue. The furnace doors opened, the heat poured out, and the faithful servants stepped in, one at a time. They thought it would be the last song they would ever hear.

THOUGHT EXERCISE

Worship is not about the music; it is about the object of worship. Is God living? Do we have images of him in our minds and love in our hearts towards him? If so, we are to do more than sing—the invitation is to worship, not create sounds. Do we set a place for him, giving him room to dwell among the people that we live with and share community? If so, we should bow before him, together, so that people know community worship. Do we offer music to him, singing songs, prophesying, and preaching his word with melodies? If so, we should also bow before him as worshipers who sing songs. To Nebuchadnezzar, the music was a prelim, like an entranceway to a higher, more dramatic venue. Notice he did not say, "Let us worship the music." Today, we preach music is our worship. Music is our venue. We sing for hours, yet in many places, no one worships. I wonder how we would respond if the doors of the furnace opened, and we had to make a choice—to bow or not to bow. Do you think someone would shout, "Can't we just sing a song?" Intimate worship brings the heat.

A Muddy Field
A Worship Story based on Hos

BUT the people of Gilead are worthless because of their idol worship, and Gilead too; they sacrifice bulls, their altars are lined up like heaps of stone along the hedges of a plowed field. (Hos 12:11).

The people had spent thousands of hard, laborious hours chiseling the stones that now lay motionless alongside the plowed fields. The rock formations had similar features, with rounded eyes, long straight noses, a rough square for heads, pitted with chisel markings, each one looking a little different than the one lying next to it. At the end of the day, the awkwardly shaped rocks bordered the field that would produce a crop of wheat. When the rains came, the people looked out over the field with desperation. Staring outward, their eyes did not focus on the heavy rocks now fully sunken into the mud, but rather at the plowed ground in hope of seeing signs of life. After several months of deferred hope, the people became like the sinking stones; they felt worthless. They, too, had sad stone faces fashioned out of dashed hopes, their smiles turned downward like the idols now buried in the mud. The people, like their idols, were useless.

THOUGHT EXERCISE

When our work becomes our worship, our works suffer, and our worship is uninhabited. God has not intended our fields of labor

Part Two: Stories of Worship

to be our act of worship. Yet, unconsciously, we insist that they are. The hours spent on planning and preparing for a meeting, rushing to plane flights, waiting in long lines to board trains or hailing taxis to get to a speaking engagement—none of it is worship. Still, to justify our sacrifice of hard labor, or inconveniences, we insist that it is. When Paul said, "I offer myself a living sacrifice" Rom 12:1, he is speaking of a real personal sacrifice, a living act of service, not an act of intimate worship. To Paul, his work was associated with the plowing of the field, like laboriously laying the groundwork for a meeting or an evangelical outreach. It is the work of ministry that Paul is referring to, not the worship of God. Review the text if you are in question.

If we insist that our service is our worship, we risk becoming like those in Gilead. This happens when our craft becomes our purpose, and our hope is in the return substance of our labor. If we are not careful, we could someday look out on our field of mission and realize that the fruit of ministry is not the reward. When life's trials come and we fail to produce the results that we ourselves have planted, we can fall into a state of worthlessness, like those in Gilead. There is, however, a way to reverse this misfortune. Do what the Bible says. Worship God and serve God, God's way. There is a spirit-filled harvest, and intimate worship produces good work.

The Last Days
A Worship Story based on Joel

"At the time of those events," says the Lord, "when I restore the captivity of Judah and Jerusalem." (Joel 3:1).

Like a wind-driven flag, jumping atop the wooden box, the man waved his arms with veracity, "There is a war coming," he shouted, "a war like no man has ever seen!" The people could see the protruding veins in his neck as his voice strained with each word. For blocks, people heard his message, and as they passed, they could not help but stop and listen to his ear-piercing speech. "In these last days I will pour out my spirit, the Lord says, and no man will escape it, these are the last days!"

Over the preacher's oration, a voice came from within the crowd, "We've heard this before. Preacher, it's doomsday!" The laughter slithered its way in and through those who had chosen to stay and watch the show. Mocking words rose, then retreated like a slow-moving tide, pulsating as a current of electricity from person to person. In spite of the ridicule, the preacher would not relent. His passion obvious, he believed the book of Joel was a message for the last days.

THOUGHT EXERCISE

There is a before and an after—we are living in the after. As Jesus said, a comforter is coming, the spirit of God will be given to all

Part Two: Stories of Worship

who believe, and if so, the after began with the words found in The Book of Acts. Just like The Book of Joel, in The Book of Acts, when the Holy Spirit's gifts began to manifest themselves in believers, the captives begin their exodus. At this time, Judah (which means praise) and Jerusalem (the altar hearth of worship), the praise and worship of God's people, enter the process of God's restorative plan. Joel is more than a doomsday trilogy; it is an announcement that the people of the world will again praise God with rich joy, and they will again worship him in intimacy. Before this rebuilding takes place, deliverance comes. Each Christian needs to understand that prior to the Holy Spirit's coming, Judah/praise was captive and Jerusalem/Ariel, the "Alter Hearth," the place where true worship was offered, had suffered violence. The Book of Joel gives us the hope that our praise will return to its fullness, and again the altar of worship will find its true meaning. Bowing down in intimate worship is a "last days" promise.

The Dysfunctional Family
A Worship Story based on Amos

"From among all the families on the earth, I have been intimate with you alone. . . .

Though this is what the Lord says to the family of Israel: 'come back to me, and live! Don't go back to the pagan altars at Bethel.'

In that day, I will restore the fallen house of David. I will repair its damaged walls. From the rooms, I will rebuild it and restore its former glory."

(Amos 3:2, 5:4, 9:11).

Through the mouth of Amos, God spoke to the Hebrew nation as if they were his only intimate family. He saw them as a unit, knit together by cultivated relationships, not only with each other, but also with their creator and deliverer, God. When his family chose Bethel over him, and the altars found there, God became a wounded family member. Pleading with them to come back, they resisted his request, and the grieving process began.

As the family grew, the depth of their sins were passed on, one to another, and then to another. The years passed, and the family suffered from dysfunctional habits. There was arguing, hatred and broken hearts from displaced children. Now, the once-perfect family struggled to survive. Then, the father made a decree: "This is going to end. I will get my family back, and it will be the family that I wanted from the beginning. Our intimacy will return."

Part Two: Stories of Worship

THOUGHT EXERCISE

In America today, statistics remind us that nearly fifty percent of all marriages end in divorce. That computes to over 2 million marriages and over 1 million divorces. That sounds staggering. However, when Amos spoke the word of the Lord to Israel, the divorce rate was nearly one hundred percent. With the exception of a few, the Hebrew families living in Bethel had divorced themselves from their first husband, Jehovah. This illegal separation created a platform of lost intimacy. Broken families bred lost worshipers. Still, God promises to rebuild lost worship, uniting his family to the "former way," not the "modern way," as we have chosen to believe in. Our first husband calls us back from Bethel, meaning that the "today way" of doing things is replaced by the "former way" of doing things, the "house of David" way. That is what God is restoring. Intimate worship leads to restoration—restoration heals the broken family.

An Old Battle
A Worship Story based on Obad

"But Jerusalem will become a refuge and for those who escape, it will be a holy place." (Obad 17).

"Both of you stop it right now! Or, I am calling your father," their mother firmly shouted.

"He started it, Mom!"

"No, I didn't, he did."

"You are such a liar!"

Taking both boys by the arm, she sternly marched the two upstairs, sitting them in their bedrooms.

"You will both sit here quietly until you apologize to each other, and I mean it!"

One boy shook his head in defiance, while the other turned toward the wall.

"Okay! That is your choice. Sit here until your father gets home, then."

The silence was unbearable. All five minutes of it. Then the feeling of idleness and the thought of not playing in the backyard wore them down. Turning slowly toward one another, they came to an agreement.

"I don't want Dad to know!"

"I don't either. Mom won't tell him if we do what she said."

"Yeah. I'm sorry."

"Me too, Let's go!"

PART TWO: STORIES OF WORSHIP

Running downstairs, they passed their mom in the kitchen as they headed out the back door.

"It's all good, Mom!"

"Yeah, thanks, Mom!"

THOUGHT EXERCISE

If it were only that easy! Jacob and Esau, Jerusalem and Edom, Jesus and King Herod, Paul or Barnabas? The spirit and the flesh, there is always conflict. How long should we preach? How many songs can we sing? Is it the pulpit, or the altar, the preacher, or the worship leader? This list keeps getting longer with each generation. Remember the resolve of the two boys: "It's all good, Mom!" Sometimes the word of the Lord comes like a child's voice, "Jerusalem, the altar, hearth" (Isa 29:2), Mount Zion, will become "a refuge"—you just have to stop fighting long enough to get there. Intimacy between brothers results in blessings from the holy place, a place where worship grows. How can we agree if we are not willing to give up our own wants? How can a person bow down at the altar with unforgiveness? Jesus said if you go to the altar and have something against a brother, you must solve it first (Matt 5:28). Like the two boys who would have to wait until the father got home, or else resolve it themselves, the Holy Spirit waits for us to relinquish our pride before the sharing of holiness found in the place of intimate worship. Solving problems leads to intimate worship.

Worship 101
A Worship Story based on Jon

Jonah answered, "I am a Hebrew, and I worship the Lord, the God of heaven, who made the sea and the land." (Jon 1:9).

"Those who worship false gods turn their backs on all of God's mercies." (Jon 2:8).

"Words matter. To understand scripture, word definitions are absolutely imperative."

Turning to the whiteboard behind him, he wrote the scriptures with such speed, it was apparent to those sitting in the room that he had presented this lesson hundreds, if not thousands of times.

Jon 1:9—YARE = fear.

Jon 2:8—SHAMAR = to keep guard.

"The biblical translations that many of you carry often transpose these two words as 'worship' in both verses. However, the use of this word, 'worship,' that we have already seen in scripture as 'Shachah' is a poor choice, a misrepresentation of the meaning of the scripture verse itself."

Several students did not know what the teacher was getting at.

"If you read Jonah 1:9, the word 'bow down' does not fit the context of the verse. The word 'fear' is a far clearer choice. Why? The sailors were in distress, the boat was in danger of being lost to the storm's force. The people on board believed that destruction came from God, and that there was a reason behind the looming disaster. After casting lots, the lots pointed to Jonah; Jonah was the object for the calamity. Knowing this, Jonah confessed his faith in hopes of saving himself. In doing this, he admits that he, too, fears God. The word that fits seamlessly in this verse is 'fear'—'Yare,' not 'Shachah,' bowing down in worship."

The students' reasoning began to sink in. One student sitting in the front row raised his hand. "So, professor, you're saying the word worship doesn't belong in this verse?"

"It's not that it doesn't belong, it is just not the best word choice. When people fear God, they will bow down, but here, bowing was not the case subject. It was the fear of the present circumstances. If Jonah would have been bowing down, or talking about doing so, the word for worship would have been found here and used in the original text."

With a glimmer of hope, the young student continued.

"In this other verse, Jon 2:8, the people were choosing to take care and guard the idols as a service to them, and that is why they lost God's favor and mercy."

"Yes," the instructor smiled. "Of course, they bowed before them, but they also spent time making sure they were in good condition. Their affections were toward their idols; thus, they have turned their backs toward God."

Before he would finish the afternoon's lessons, the teacher paused, hoping there would be a few more questions. After several minutes of contemplation, he concluded, "Words matter. If a person says, 'I am a worshiper of God,' they need to actually worship to make it a true confession."

Closing his notes, the instructor walked towards the door.

"When was the last time you worshiped God according to his definition of worship? Do not forget about the words for worship assignment. See you next week."

THOUGHT EXERCISE

Words make a difference. Knowing what word fits where and how to use them creatively is a gift, but it is also a discipline. 2 Tim

2:15 tells us to handle the words found in scripture correctly, study them, know what the words mean. Do not make things up or base your belief on old stories. The word *worship* has a definite root meaning; when you learn what it is, it will lead you to true intimate times of clearly understood worship. When was the last time you invested yourself in worship, God's way?

A Simple Plan
A Worship Story based on Mic

"What can we bring to the Lord? What kind of offerings should we give him? Should we bow before God with offerings of yearling calves?" (Mic 6:6).

The staff meeting began as it typically did. A few jokes, a short prayer for the needs of some of its members, but around the table, it was business as usual. The lead person asked the common questions about the attendants, and the Sunday school, and shared his feelings about the flow of the service. He pointed out what went smoothly and what things needed tightening up. There was always something to work on. After a few comments and suggestions, plans for the next week's service was the final topic. The order of things each week depended on guest speakers and special music, but for the most part, the direction of service was unchanged.

It began with a short hello, several songs, then a break to greet one another. Next came a short sermon on giving, and then the main sermon. In conclusion, the altar call was open as people waited near the front to pray. To make for a clean outro, a few more songs played as the people quietly dismissed. Overall, it was a simple plan.

Then, the new pastor, the one who had just come on board, raised his hand and asked the question, "Are we sure that this is what the Lord wants for next week's service?"

With rolling of eyes and a covered cough or two, the leaders sitting at the table silently pondered the young pastor's question.

A Simple Plan

One man looked at the man sitting next to him, and the next one looked to the next one to him. When it came to the head chair, the room was silent, each eye focused on the lead man. "Well, I know this all is new to you, but this is the way we do it. I am sure God is okay with it. Why would he reinvent the wheel? If it works, why change it? You know what I mean, right?"

Like a punctured balloon, the young man's spirit sank into nothing. "Oh, of course, I guess you're right," the young minister replied.

THOUGHT EXERCISE

We need to be cautious not to replace the Holy Spirit's works with a humanistic form of spiritual government. This simply translates to, "The work of men cannot replace the work of God." There was a time in church history when the government of the Holy Spirit was priority, but that has been long lost. Today, people do not ask; they tell. They tell us what words we can be saying, what songs should be sung, when our time is up, and where things such as prayer belong in the list of service events. They even go as far as to tell us how much time we have in God's presence. In most meetings today, the clock is the ruling factor, as is the pressure to perform for the purpose of acceptance. Today people's happiness is the tool for monitoring success, and so the wheel of man-guided spiritual government continues to turn with little effort. It is easy to follow the formula, even when it is older than the people who use it.

At least the lost people of Israel had the intuitiveness to pose the questions, "What can we bring?" "Should we bow down?"

In the deviant condition that the Hebrew people were in at the time of Micah, even they had the sense that God had wants, that he had feelings and thoughts, and most of all, he desired more than a formulated service. As church community leaders, we lay out our service plans like a string of beads, placing the right color in just the right place. We have done it so many times, we know exactly what will be pleasing to those who come to look at this

Part Two: Stories of Worship

finely crafted ornament. Yet, in our great expertise, which one of us asks the question, "Should we bow down?"

Worship service after worship service, and no one worships. "Do you think we should at least ask?"

Could we be afraid of the answer? God is not mundane, or repetitious; he does not think like us. He said, "No!" to the nation of Israel, but at least they asked the question.

We say, "No!" before asking.

If someone does ask, intimate worship is more than a planned service.

The Lost City
A Worship Story based on Nah

And this is what the Lord says concerning the Assyrians in Nineveh. "You will have no more children to carry on your name. I will destroy all the idols in the temples of your gods. I am preparing a grave for you because you are despicable." (Nah 1:14).

Nineveh, the city Jonah visited one hundred years prior, was once a place of revived hearts and refreshed souls. Now, it received a word of destruction from the modern prophet, Nahum. One of the oldest cities in antiquity, the largest and most well-protected community was secured only by its thick walls and multitude of high towers. So strong was the metropolitan capital city of Assyria, it proudly feared no one, not foreign gods or kings. Nineveh, the self-sufficient one, content with its commerce, trade, political rule, and self-government, had achieved a sphere of success. Considered safe from the outside world, Nineveh was living on its reservoir of pride. Safe, perhaps from the neighboring competition, but not so from the Lord of heaven's armies. Nineveh, shortly after Nahum's word of judgment, became a grave buried deep beneath the ground without a gravestone.

THOUGHT EXERCISE

What makes a city great? Is it the location? The strength of its walls and fortifications? Is a city boundless because of its wealth and

Part Two: Stories of Worship

commerce? Does fair human rights, correct politics and stable government make a city prodigious? Of course not! What makes a city great is what Nineveh was lacking: intimate worship with an intimate God.

Heb 12 says we have come to a city built on heaven's countenance, the city where all know how to worship with intimacy. This city is not in heaven alone, but exists on earth, in us. Thus, we need not be like Nineveh, but rather, like the heavenly Jerusalem, the city of the living God, whose concerns are for the altar of worship and what happens there. Unlike Nineveh, true worshipers will not be lost to an unmarkable tombstone but measured alive by the crown of Christ. This is reason enough to intimately bow before the king of the city.

Casting Out an Image
A Worship Story based on Hab

"What good is an idol carved by man or a cast image that teaches lies? How foolish to trust in your own creation—a god that cannot even talk! What sorrows awaits you who say to wooden idols, 'Wake up and save us!' To speechless stone images, you say, 'rise up and teach us!' Can an idol tell you what to do?"
(Hab 2:18–20).

He walked into the room an unknown pastor with extreme gifts of discernment. There he saw the teenage boy lying flat on his bed, his eyes glazed, his forehead shining from sweat. Looking around, the pastor noticed the pictures hanging above the bed, and the beaded necklace hanging over the doorway, and by the window perched a crucifixion. Before entering the boy's room, the spiritual man reflected on the statues hovering above the fireplace, and another in the hallway.

The porcelain figurines had painted faces, wearing long robes, holding up outstretched arms, as if to invite someone in. During the several hours that followed, the preacher at one point told everyone who was standing there watching that he wanted all the idols taken outside and thrown away. "These things are a lie," he ordered. The night wore on, and many earth-shaking events transpired. Those who had the nerve to stay and watch were shocked by what took place. Several days after, the teenage boy gathered himself and started a new journey in life without the lying spirits and the lifeless idols that had taunted him in the past. Now he walked free.

THOUGHT EXERCISE

In the world in which we live, learning takes place in a multitude of ways. Seeing, feeling, listening, touching, and doing, all of these are tools that teach. You might think that a lifeless piece of porcelain in the shape of a man or a woman is harmless, but if it were no threat, God would had never bothered with it. Idols would never have been banned from the presence of God if they were good things. God is alert to all our senses, and knows what teaches our spirits truth, and what teaches lies. Statues carved thousands of years ago are no different from those constructed today. They teach people falsehoods, and falsehoods keep us from knowing the real God. Even when the idols sit silently on our walls, above our beds and next to our windows, they represent a teaching that is far from true worship. This is a basic truth, if you want to worship God intimately you will have to throw out your old, past idols. Intimate worship has no room for figurines.

Rooftop
A Worship Story based on Zeph

"For they go up to their roof's and bow down to the sun, moon and stars. They claim to follow the Lord, but then they worship Molech, too. And I will destroy those who used to worship me, but no longer do." (Zeph 1:5-6).

Looking up at the stars, the young boy lying flat on his bed felt the cold air settling on his face. Since he was a child, the rooftop had been his bedroom and here, he learned to love his privacy, as the rest of his family, including his brother-in-law, and their three children lived below on the bottom floor. Each evening, if it was not raining or too windy and cold, he lay on his small bed, staring into the heavens, wondering. "I know there is a God," he whispered. "But who is he?"

His family did not believe the way the Hebrew people did, but similarly. His father spoke of more than one God, while the boy's mother believed in just one, like his sister and her husband.

However, the boy did not like the name Molech. He often thought, *Where did that name come from, anyway?* "I kind of like the sound of the Hebrews' God, Jehovah," he whispered, not wanting anyone to hear. To the boy, the Hebrew name sounded more like a god who could do things for people. "Jehovah, Jehovah," he said several times, as if trying on a new pair of shoes. "It sounds bigger than Molech." As the starlight crossed overhead, the shape of the sparkling white lights was a beautiful canvas in motion. As heaven's hue turned shades of dark purple and then deep black, the boy's eyes began to uncontrollably close. "I want to worship the real God," he said, reaching his hands towards the stars. Rolling out of his bed, he kneeled on the stone rooftop, both hands on the ground and his face looking upward. "Maybe my brother-in-law is right!" With his face touching the ground, he whispered to the stars. "Molech, Molech."

THOUGHT EXERCISE

We have all done it—wondered to ourselves in private, "Who is He?" If we ask people that question, we will hear several different answers. When we read Genesis 4, we find the first-time people actually called out the name of God together, and the name was not Molech! Like back then, today there is only one: his name is Jesus, and whether on a rooftop in a foreign land or in a church gathering on Sunday morning, his true name deserves our true intimate worship.

A Short Memory
A Worship Story based on Hag

"Does anyone remember this house—this Temple—in its former splendor? How, in comparison, does it look to you now?" (Hag 2:3).

For the first time in many years, they were free. Free people who could do whatever they wanted, whenever they wanted. Their liberation had come to them without any doing of their own. At the beginning, they considered the one who had led them into their freedom, but not too long after, their attention turned. Soon, white stone buildings spotted the landscape, surrounded by fields blooming with wheat, as sheep and cattle grazed the open areas. The people were free to set their own rules, and they governed themselves the way they wanted to govern. They had money, and food, and plenty of it; still, they never felt as if it were enough. Then the word of the Lord through Haggai came to them: "Does anyone remember the former house?" After the temple's destruction, all that had been rebuilt was the foundation of the past temple. They had accomplished that, but all else was forgotten. No one wanted to work on the interior parts of the former house. The people were more interested in their own personal residence. The community had become more important than the relationship with their God, just as their politics and commerce had consumed them. The personal places of God were not important anymore. Without seeing it, their newfound freedom became a second bondage. The comparison between the temple of God and their own lives was

PART TWO: STORIES OF WORSHIP

clearly obtrusive. So perplexing were the prophets' questions and the problem in front of them, it took a sovereign move by God to restore the residence where intimate worship would take place. Instead of waiting for the people to remember the former house, God moved on them with great enthusiasm as the work on the temple began again.

THOUGHT EXERCISE

Israel's past holds keys to a successful future. When we see ourselves as a free people in Christ, we then must ask the question, "What do we do with our freedom?" Do we build homes for ourselves, communities based on beliefs and traditions? Is our freedom a "get out of jail free card," allowing us to live any way that best suits us, benefiting us physically and morally? What is our Christ-bought freedom about? Like the tribe of Judah, overtaken by their liberty, investing all their time on new houses, cities, and governments, have we done the same in this present world? During our free time, have we neglected the temple of God, the altar where true worship takes place?

In this verse, what is important to see is the prophet was not angry about what the Hebrews had built, but rather, discomforted over what they had not built. The lesson learned is that God is more concerned about worship than politics, community living, commerce, and civil rights. If there is no worship, none of it matters. You can blame it on a short memory, but what will not change is the fact that the former house is greater than any present man-made house. Even more important, what took place in the former temple house is what God expects from the future temple house. To worship intimately, surrounded by the Lord's presence, is God's main objective. This goal supersedes all the good constructive works. Intimate worship is the framework for the former, present, and future house. Intimate worship is worth remembering.

Getting It Straight
A Worship Story based on Zech

When I looked again, I saw a man with a measuring line in his hand. "Where are you going?" I asked.

He replied, "I am going to measure Jerusalem, to see how wide and how long it is." (Zech 2:1).

"A plumb line cannot lie," the man said, dropping his line down from the top of the wall to the dirt below. "If this is straight, everything is good!" The master builder's hands were hard looking, like the bricks that he carried. Gripping the edges with each finger, lifting the stone up into place, laying it squarely in position took practice, as well as a strong forearm.

The young apprentice saw his power, and while watching from behind began to doubt if he could do the job.

"It's all about the line. Remember, keep it absolutely straight. If it is not, I will see it, and you will have to start over—from the bottom up!" The man's face, like his arms and neck, were weatherbeaten, with deep wrinkles across his forehead and around his eyes. His voice was rough.

The apprentice had just finished digging. It was a tough way to make a living, taking its toll on the human body. By the end of the day, the young man questioned if this job was for him; it had been much harder than he thought. After a long day of rough work, he looked at the elongated brick wall with one eye closed, trying to see anything that looked like a flaw. With a last glance, he could see it was perfectly straight, without a waver or curve; not

Part Two: Stories of Worship

one brick was out of place. Something settled in the young man's stomach. "I think the line worked!" As he wound up the line, putting it in his new tool bag, he smiled. "Maybe I can do this job. I just need to keep my eye on the line."

THOUGHT EXERCISE

What does a plumb line have to do with worship? In Zachariah 2:1, the prophet is describing how meticulous God is about the offering of worship. Not only is he pointing to Jerusalem, Arial, the altar hearth, the place of worship, he is measuring its depth by precise increments. How crazy is that! God is looking deep into the molecular structure that is the foundation of his most holy place, a city where people, by grace, come to worship. If the inhabitants of this worship place knew how definitive God was about worship, and how keenly he investigated the inner structure, I do not know if they would want to go there.

Like the young apprentice, it first appears too difficult. Bowing down and worshiping in any situation takes strategic planning, a clear view of God's blueprints, and a measuring tool. God not only warns us in the book of Zechariah prior to his inspection, he repeats himself again in Revelation 11:1. "Then there was given me a measuring rod like a staff; and someone said, get up and measure the temple of God, and the altar, and those who worship in it." Why would God measure the depth of worship with a plumb line? The answer is simple. The true temple of worship rises-up one brick at a time. If it is not plumb, it will not last. Not only will it eventually crumble, having to be rebuilt, but it will also not line up with its counterpart, the heavenly Jerusalem. See Hebrews 12. How deep is our worship? How long? The master builder is coming to inspect it, so be ready. Intimate worship will be measured.

The Vow

A Worship Story based on Mal

"Judah has been unfaithful, and a detestable thing has been done in Israel and in Jerusalem. The men of Judah have defiled the Lord's beloved sanctuary by marrying women who worship idols." (Mal 2:11).

"To have and to hold, through sickness and health, rich or poor, until death do you part. You may kiss the bride." With both hands carefully on her waist, her arms hanging gently over his shoulders, they kissed, softly. The intimate moment sealed the vow and before all watching, including their Creator, the commitment was consecrated. Marriage is for life.

Backpack in hand, he slammed the door behind him as he walked to his car. It was six years after the vow, and today, both were calling it quits. What they had in common at the beginning was no longer. Ideas, once seemingly similar, were miles apart. What one believed in, the other did not, and the foundation of faith that should have supported them, sank like wet sand during the incoming tide. Starting his car, he looked back one more time, just hoping that maybe she would open the front door. "I wish someone would have warned me," he said, then drove slowly away.

Part Two: Stories of Worship

THOUGHT EXERCISE

A broken marriage, even though commonly accepted today, is a sad thing. Aside from who did wrong or who did right, the real damage is internal, unseen—not only by the broken couple, but also by those who publicly witnessed the exchange of vows. The effects of divorce sink deep into a person's soul, laying silent like a submerged explosive mine, just waiting for the right moment, then erupting from beneath the surface. Very few escape the collateral damage of such an explosion.

After such an event, the words heard most often are, "I wish someone would have warned me!" Thoughtfully, would they have listened if someone had warned them? Did they want to hear the words, "This is not the right one," or "You have nothing in common, nothing long-term!" Weeks before the wedding, would it have done any good to say, "This is a bad idea, don't do it"?

Since the creation of Adam, the problem remains. No one wants to hear it. Still, God says it anyway. "Don't go there!"

It is not just individuals who refuse to listen. It is cities, countries and nations who refuse to hear it as well. "Don't join those who worship idols, the sanctuary is too precious to me." That is what God says. We are too precious to him. Intimate worship cannot be shared with people who have nothing in common with it or have no similar ideas or foundation. 2 Corinthians 6:14 says in the King James version, "be ye not an equally yoked." The word is saying, do not bind yourselves together with a man or a woman who is not a believer. The apostle is clearly making a statement: "it is dangerous." Malachi is saying the same thing.

Of course, we have a mission and responsibility to impart the message of his saving grace to the men and women around us, but this mission is not worship—worship is not a mission. Instead of trying to understand what God is saying about the place of worship, we invite the world into his sanctuary, making room for those who are apathetic, those who are not interested. When we gather, our rule is to make it comfortable for the visitor, saved or not, with the hope that they will return. Then, to serve the world, we attach ourselves to things outside the true sanctuary, like idols, moral issues, political agendas—things having nothing to do with the government of God. When this happens, tolerance, in the broad-minded sense, is waiting for us like a bride looking for a groom to stroll peacefully down the aisle of union. If we are not mindful, the wedding vow sealed with a kiss in the sanctuary of intimate worship will run the course of divorce. The warning is given! Likened to a marriage, intimate worship has only one true lover: Jesus. Rom 14:11 says this: "every knee will bow." Intimate worship is a vow not to be broken.

Part Two: Stories of Worship

A Short History Lesson

In the chapters of the Old Testament books, Genesis to Malachi, the word "worship" in Hebrew, "Shachah," simply means to "bow face down." With the coming of Alexander, the Great and his conquest of the known world, the Torah, the five books of the Hebrew nation, experiences a God encounter. I say "God encounter" for the fact that God allowed the Hebrew and Greek cultures to collide. This brought about a cross-pollination of written languages. The silent years between the Old Testament and the New Testament were not so silent, for God was translating his prophetic word into a language that the whole world would soon be able to read. This translation has had an everlasting profound impact on world history. The word for "worship," once "Shachah," found in the Hebrew language, now in Greek, was "Proskyneo," meaning to "*bow down, kissing, as a dog who licks his master's hand.*" Together in one book, the two words, "Shachah" and "Proskyneo," paint a complete picture of what Jesus, in John 4:24, titles "True Worship." This is where we start in the New Testament, beginning with the book of Matt. Now the word is "Proskyneo."

The True Gift
A Worship Story based on Matt 2

AFTER they had heard the king, they started out. The star they had seen rising led them until it stopped over the place where the child was. They were overwhelmed with joy to see the star. When they entered the house, they saw the child with his mother, Mary. So, they bowed down and worshiped him. Then, they opened their treasure chests and offered him gifts of gold, frankincense, and myrrh. (Matt 2:11).

The word from the king was simple: "Go find them!" Yet, the intent behind the words came filled with alternative plans. The three men could not get out of there fast enough, and leaving the city behind brought relief, for they had escaped with their lives and were now joined on a mission that seemed worthwhile. Each night, as they looked up at the star overhead, the feeling of destiny was unexplainable. Who or what lay ahead, the men could not imagine. They expected it to be human, not an angel or anything of that sort, but they still did not know. Was it a god they were looking for, or an earthlike king? They planned on a king; they had never seen a god before.

Following the guideposts, the search for this newborn led them in a straight line. It was a direct path, a GPS route as seen from heaven's window. From a human perspective, the route they were following was full of steep, sandy hills and tight, turning pathways. From overhead, in the air, it was a straight line, an easy course to traverse.

Anticipation turned to joy as the shining object in the sky stopped and hovered quietly over the place where the mission would end. Holding gifts, they quietly entered the room, and seeing the child, they laid their gifts to one side. The journey was about this moment. Facedown in the straw, they worshiped intimately. Later that day, they opened the presents.

THOUGHT EXERCISE

When I first heard this story, it was the baby in the manger and then the gifts offered to the child that caught my attention. The amazing journey and the expensive offerings, to me, were the epicenter of this historical moment. Today, I see it differently. The journey of the three men was God's uninterrupted prophetic roadmap unfolding before the world's eyes, as a testimony to God's redemptive plan for humanity. The gifts presented in honor of the heavenly King were the reflection of heaven's precious purity lying there in bodily form.

On a personal level, I have adopted the journey and the desire to pursue the king of creation. The gifts he received, he somehow bestowed on me (Ephesians 4:8). However, do I want to reciprocate to the degree that I would be willing to lay the gifts aside and simply bow, intimately worshiping the Savior of the world? Intimate worship is the real gift, a gift more costly than a good journey for high-priced, carefully wrapped benevolences. The child in the manger was not aware of either one, but all heaven rejoiced when the travelers bowed intimately before the newborn king. I hope my journey will produce the same.

The Flock
A Worship Story based on Matt 8

WHEN Jesus came down from the mountain, large crowds followed him. A man with a serious skin disease came and bowed down in front of him. The man said to Jesus, "Sir, if you're willing, you can make me clean." (Matt 8:2).

Like a flock of seagulls hovering over a live fish stranded on the beach, squawking at one another, pecking and flapping their wings with animosity, so these people amorously scurried down the hillside following his footsteps. He did not look back; he knew who was there. He could hear the religious men with questions, the women who wanted another look at his face, and the younger ones who came for the excitement and experience.

Yet, within that hectic colony of gulls, a few, deeply serious and in search of more than a religious answer or exciting encounter, waited patiently. As the crowd descended the hillside, the quiet ones fell towards the back of the congregation. They were insecure in themselves, not wanting anyone to cast attention in their direction. When the moment presented itself, the man who no one wanted to touch walked through the crowd of squawking fowl. Finding his way before the one whom he had been following all that morning, he drew a deep breath. His words, humbly spoken, were short and to the point. His eyes had a desperate glaze as he stood, unsure, expecting no favors, but only for a moment. Finding himself in God's presence, the truth surfaced—it was not about his need. It was about publicly worshiping intimately, so he did. The healing came later.

THOUGHT EXERCISE

Sometimes, to me, the gathering of saints resembles a flock of seagulls. Frantically, they chatter without pause, hysterically looking for the most advantageous position, just to get a good morsel of truth. They flap their wings as they fight one another and hope to hold the ground that will provide the best results. "Be in the front!" they squawk. "There is more anointing near the front!"

When the crazed flock gathers, they make it difficult for the weaker ones to get past the human obstacles. Standing in the way of those who are weaker, the noisy birds proudly demonstrate their spirituality in the form of chaotic activity, fluttering their wings harmoniously as they try to raise themselves to a higher perch. Nevertheless, the Holy Spirit of God hovers over it all. He sees the man pecking his way through the masses with honorable intentions, and he waits for him. God is bigger than the drove of wild birds. Those who come to God thinking about their need, often find intimate worship in place of medicinal relief. Come to think about it, I have never seen a congregation of seagull's worship face-down with intimacy. Jesus did heal the man, but it was later, after he had finished worshiping.

SHOREVIEW

A Worship Story based on Matt 14

JESUS said, "Come!" So, Peter got out of the boat and walked on the water towards Jesus. But when he noticed how strong the wind was, he became afraid and started to sink. He shouted, "Lord, save me!" Immediately, Jesus reached out, caught hold of him and said, "You have so little faith! Why did you doubt?" When they got into the boat, the wind stopped blowing. The man in the boat bowed down in front of Jesus and said, "You are truly the son of God." (Matt 14:29-33).

When he was a boy, the sandy shores were his playground. As a young man, the white-capped waterway stretching across the horizon was his workplace. Now, too old to haul nets, he fished, but only in his late-night dreams. When the dreams came, he could feel the water pushing the boat side to side, splashing over the rails, the wind pressing against his face. Even in his sleep, his forearms tightened as he gripped the invisible ropes, pulling in the sails, fighting to balance the keel against the intrusive current. Once out of harm's way, sailing peacefully onto the shore, the dream always ended the same: laughing children, with their hands outstretched, running up to the boat full of fish. Handing the fish to as many as he could, his heart was joyful, knowing he had done something worthwhile. The dreams were now a good part of his life, like the early morning walk on the beach.

On that morning, the wind was exceptionally strong. In the distance, he saw a small boat, moving up and then down,

Part Two: Stories of Worship

disappearing below larger swells, then appearing again. From his viewpoint on the beach, the man noticed something odd. There was someone standing next to the wave-tossed vessel. Wrinkling his brow, squinting as if looking into the hot sun, he could not believe what he was seeing. One of the men who had been sitting in the boat stepped over the railing and into the water.

Panic filled the old man's chest. "This should not be happening," he shouted. Running up to the top of the sand berm, he could see everything. "This is unexplainable," he said, waving his arms in distress. "Get back in the boat, you fool!" His voice died against the wind.

As if hearing the man's words, both men stepped back into the safety of the watertight hull. With a short sigh of relief, the onlooker watched as all those in the boat disappeared, yet again, but not behind the waves, for the wind had suddenly abated and the waves were no more. "What are they doing now?" he grumbled. "Why are they bowing down like that? They must have an idol on board, or they have seen a god!"

That evening, when he had fallen into a deep sleep, the man had another dream. Instead of pulling ropes and casting nets, he saw a ghost-like person walking on the white-capped sea. With his hand stretched out, the man-shaped spirit whispered, "Come with me."

First with one foot and then another, he stepped over the railing and instantly began to sink into the rough waters. Violently, the dream ended. Before his eyes could see clearly, the man knew in his spirit that the dream was from God. Next to his bed, he carefully lowered himself to the ground, worshiping intimately before the God who had walked among the waves.

THOUGHT EXERCISE

Doesn't it all depend on a person's perspective? From one point, something looks one way, and from another point, that same thing looks like something else. So, can anyone have the one true perspective on anything? In this story, is it the old fishermen on the beach, or would it be those in the boat that had the true perspective? I would put my money on those sitting in the boat.

I heard a man say that he felt closer to God when he was out fishing on a lake than when he was sitting in church. I laughed at that. I know it is much more peaceful and without all the busyness going on; it is quieter out on the water fishing then sitting through a church service. So, from his perspective, I would agree. I would suggest if he lowered himself on his face to worship God intimately while fishing in his boat, he should be careful not to snag himself on a hook, or even worse, fall overboard. At least if you bow down in a church service, you are most likely not going to have a boating accident. From my perspective, it is safer to worship on dry land.

A Talented Mom
A Worship Story based on Matt 20

THEN the mother of Zebedee's sons came to Jesus with her two sons. She bowed down in front of him to ask him for a favor. "What do you want?" He asked her. (Matt 20:20).
"I want your hair washed, your teeth brushed . . . and good, too!"
Quickly, she piled the two boys' clothes on their bed. Laying them out in perfect order, she looked for any stains or wrinkles. Lifting each one, smelling them for fish, she set aside the cleanest pair. All the time they spent with their father fishing had ruined nearly every piece of nice clothing they had. But, today was the day, and she wanted everything in perfect order.
As if on a mission, the woman marched through the streets, her two boys close behind, moving in perfect step with their mother, who quickly zigzagged from corner to corner. Without looking back, she benevolently gave her instructions. "Don't slouch! Keep your shoulders back and stomach in. If he asks you anything the answer is, 'Yes sir,' or 'No sir.' No silly remarks!"
Both boys rolled their eyes.
"And no mumbling, that's the worst thing you can do! Your father mumbles," she mumbled.
Nearly eighteen, having worked in their father's fishing business since they could walk, both had long been accomplished anglers, stern and confident. Still, when their mother was close, both boys surrendered to her compassionate leadership.

A Talented Mom

"I won't settle for just anything, so if he gets angry, let him." Stopping in the middle of the street, wagging her finger at her two boys, she said, "And remember, good things come to those who use a little persuasion."

She knew the protocol: respectful, bowing, so that is what she did. Respectful bowing with a positive attitude, and he just might grant her request.

Before she could get up off the ground, Jesus knew her thoughts and her questions. It was not the bowing that mattered to Jesus—he could see through all of that. It was her hidden agenda catching his attention.

With seemingly little effort, Jesus posed the question, as if saying, "What do you really, really want?" The two boys stood as the mother had commanded; both stood in silence, trying not to make eye contact, as they did not want to answer any questions.

THOUGHT EXERCISE

Most mothers have a natural ability to gather, prepare, and organize, and those who have the talent deserve high honor and respect. Getting the kids ready for church every Sunday has purpose and reward, knowing that God rewards those who diligently seek and serve him. That is a good thing to remember when pulling the car out of the driveway, twenty minutes late, with thoughts of, "I think I forgot something! Did I leave the stove on?"

For a mother, knowing that her children have found Jesus is her reward, making the hard work worth every moment. They might not be standing tall with perfectly clean clothes or even answering all the questions correctly, but at least they are there acknowledging the door to heaven. Mothers should feel proud when their kids stand firm, accepting their mission in life, even if it takes a little organized persuading on her part. Nonetheless, there is a danger. Being so organized and so focused on the practical, you can miss the important moments in life.

This is what happened to the mother who took her two boys to see Jesus. Jesus was interested in the two boys, soon to be disciples;

PART TWO: STORIES OF WORSHIP

he had big plans for them, but he was also deeply concerned about her. Being more anxious about the fate of her two sons, she failed to worship Jesus, God's way. She had the form, but not the focus. The lesson in this story is, anyone can bow. However, bowing with alternative motives invites probing questions.

A Drowsy Spirit
A Worship Story based on Matt 26

THEN, Jesus went with the disciples to a place called Gethsemane. He said to them, "Stay here while I go over there and pray." He took Peter and Zebedee's two sons with him. He was beginning to feel deep anguish. Then he said to them, "My anguish is so great that it feels as if I'm dying. Wait here and stay awake with me." After walking a little further, he quickly bowed with his face to the ground and prayed. "Father, if it is possible that this cup of suffering be taken away from me. But let your will be done rather than mine." (Matt 26:38–39).

Looking at one another, the two young men both thought the same thing. "Mom would be so proud of us!"

But when they heard his words, "I feel as if I am dying," their self-confidence turned into absolute terror.

"What does he mean ... dying?" The younger boy looked at his brother and asked the question with timidity. "Dying?"

"Don't mumble!" The older boy replied, "You sound like dad."

The two brothers gravitated to the only secure person they knew. Peter.

"Sit down, both of you. It's going to be a long night," Peter said, resting himself against a large stone. Soon asleep, the three knew little of what was taking place. Even when Jesus returned, giving them definite directions, the power needed to keep them out of that drowsy state could not be summoned. They all missed it, and the boy's mother would soon hear all about it.

Part Two: Stories of Worship

THOUGHT EXERCISE

I had a person tell me once that he never read the verse in the Bible that said, Jesus worshiped. "Why would Jesus do that?" he questioned.

At first, his statement caught me off guard. Then, knowing that I would have to walk him through it, one verse at a time, I accepted the challenge.

When I was finished with the quick Bible lesson, the man still did not believe it, nor did he want to discuss it.

It is so simple: whatever Jesus has done, we also need to do. That includes praying, preaching, sharing the gospel, feeding the hungry and healing the sick. For some reason, some people never quite get to the intimate worship part. Could it be they have a drowsy spirit?

A Short Sprint
A Worship Story based on Matt 28:8-9

THEY hurried away from the tomb with fear and great joy and ran to tell his disciples. Suddenly, Jesus met them and greeted them. They went up to him, bowed down to worship him, and took hold of his feet. (Matt 28:8–9).

"Run! Faster!" Mary shouted. At first, the stones under their feet had no effect, but soon, each stride was bruising pain. "Keep running!" Her voice echoed off the shiny round stones beneath her feet. Pushing them on was the fearful encounter, mixed with the joy of the revelation miracle. Jesus had risen!

Over, and around, up a slope and then down again the stone-laden road showed no end in sight. Their lungs burning from lack of air, their tired legs beginning to slow, they pushed on. Then, with great relief, they saw in front of them an oasis. It was the breath of life, the living Word standing in their path. Before finishing his greeting, they fell on the ground, holding his feet with tired, winded, intimate worship.

THOUGHT EXERCISE

When was the last time you felt the fear and the joy of being a Christian, all at one time? Do you remember the joyful times? How about moments of captivating fear; any of those? Have you ever felt the pain of running a hard, short sprint, the burning down in the

Part Two: Stories of Worship

lungs, the short, intermittent breaths, accompanied by pain in the lower calves? If you have, you will never forget the feeling. Have you ever felt like running to tell someone about an experience that you just had? If the answer is no, what about this question: When was the last time you bowed down joyfully, fearfully, intimately, grasping for the feet of your resurrected Savior, God, Jesus? For those who do not like to exercise, you do not have to run to get there; intimate worship is right below your feet.

Bad Eggs

A Worship Story based on Matt 28:16

THE eleven disciples went to the mountain of Galilee where Jesus had told them to go. When they saw him, they bowed down in worship, though some had doubts. (Matt 28:16).

"Why would he want us to walk all the way here?" the man complained.

"I don't know," the one next to him replied with a sharp tongue. "I am sure he has a good reason."

"What kind of reason? There is nothing here, just sharp rocks and weeds; there is nowhere to sit!"

"Stop complaining, we don't have to have a reason."

"A fool does not have a reason, that's why he is a fool!" the complainer shouted.

"Stop the negative talk, it's making things worse."

"I doubt it could get any worse!"

THOUGHT EXERCISE

Ever had this conversation? *Why are we doing this? Why should we go there? Why should we listen to this?* Just in case no one has told you, not every idea is a good idea. People have plenty of good ideas, but just as many unproductive ones. You should watch out for those. When someone tells you to do something, there is nothing wrong with asking why, if it is done respectfully.

PART TWO: STORIES OF WORSHIP

Being in a group makes for harder decision-making, especially for those who have a difficult time speaking up in a crowd. Those who quietly doubt usually go unnoticed, with one exception. When it comes to intimate worship, bowing down with a questionable heart can draw attention from God. He is big on the hearts that doubt, or ones that hide secrets.

I know people stand and sing without really meaning it. It is easy for our minds to drift off while our lips are singing hymns of praise. Jesus said, "With your mouth, you say one thing, but your hearts are far off." I totally get that! In church, when I sit for too long, I sometimes disconnect, especially if the speaker is long-winded. Yet, when I am bowing down on my face, there is no way I am going to be thinking of something else, and I am not doing it just because the crowd is telling me to. Come to think of it, I have never seen a crowd bow down all at once, at least not where I live.

THE STRONG WIND
A Worship Story based on Mark 7:25

IN fact, as soon as she heard about it, a woman whose little daughter was possessed by an impure spirit came and fell at his feet. (Mark 7:25).

Her heart was at the point of breaking when she realized modern means could not solve her problem. No one had the solution for how her child was acting. Uncontrollable surges of anger, defiance, outbreaks of screaming and crying—it was unnatural, unlike any other child she knew. Then she heard a secret from a friend; Jesus was coming to a house nearby, and she made plans to be there. Nothing would stop this woman; she was full of force and relentless in her pursuit of the answer. Like a strong wind beating upon the door of a house, she rushed towards Jesus, falling at his feet.

THOUGHT EXERCISE

Not all acts of bowing are worship. In this story, the woman threw herself at Jesus like a storm wind beating against a house. (That is the Greek meaning of the word "fell down.") Not a word was said about worship. Matter of fact, this public demonstration had nothing to do with worship, but rather supplicating for a need. Throwing one's self down exposes the level of desperation, not necessarily the depth of love. Later, when her anxiousness subsided and her daughter was healed, the women could have had a moment of reflecting in a private time of worship, or a quiet moment of thankfulness, perhaps. Intimate worship is often born during these times of rest, but it is the moments when all hell is breaking loose that we come to a place where nothing matters other than seeing Jesus and supplicating at his feet. Exasperated or not, throwing one's self down like a wind-driven rage before the creator of all things is a good place to be, and when coupled with worship is powerful. True, intimate worship, like a raging wind, is a force of its own.

A Prestigious Guest
A Worship Story based on Luke 7:44-46

THEN he turned toward the woman and said to Simon, "Do you see this woman? I came into your house, you did not give me any water for my feet, but she wet my feet with her tears and wiped them with her hair. You did not give me a kiss, but this woman, from the time I entered, has not stopped kissing my feet. You did not put oil on my head, but she has poured perfume on my feet."
(Luke 7:44-46).

As he spoke, the man glanced down to see the woman curled up on the floor, covering his guest's feet with her long brown hair. A hint of embarrassment rolled over him like a cold rush of air as his spirit felt a sharp quiver. With the bowl of water out of reach and the vase of oil sitting empty, Simon thought that maybe he could quickly grab it, undoing what he had done, but it was too late. This was Jesus, the son of Mary, his prestigious guest, yet Simon had failed to give him the honor due his name. Despite his forgetfulness, the smell of perfume hovered in the air as the people who entered were enticed by the sweet fragrance.

Nervously, Simon looked again at the woman bowing at the feet of Jesus. At first his feelings were that of resentment; she was drawing all the attention to herself, he thought. Then, suddenly, his antipathy softened. Seeing the tears running over and down the feet of Jesus, accompanied by the sounds of weeping as it rose into the air like a bouquet of fine scent, it all made sense to him. The cleansing water resting in the silver bowl by the front door was

PART TWO: STORIES OF WORSHIP

nothing compared to the tears dripping from the woman's face. The oil that he should have poured over Jesus's head was symbolic, nothing equal to the perfume the woman held in her hands. Glancing about the room, seeing all who had come to mingle and talk, the host of the house stepped back, giving true worship its place.

THOUGHT EXERCISE

We invite Jesus to every gathering, yet we misidentify the purpose of his coming, making limited room for worshipers to worship. The displacement of worship by social collaboration comes about when the bowl of cleansing water holds higher honor, as does the bottle of anointing oil, thus the personal act of worship goes undetected. The symbolism of worship holds higher status than the actual occurrence, and like Simon, we are unable to ascertain true worship, even when it is in our own home. When the true posture of worship is realized, grasping for a bottle of water and a small vial of oil will not meet the need. Entering the room, Jesus becomes the altar of worship, and the worshiper transforms into the water and the oil as they lay themselves at his feet. This is more than metaphorical; it is an unpretentious demonstration of acknowledgment in real time. Worship is not a figurative word; it is as real as the water we drink, and the oil that we use to soften our skin. Intimate worship carries substance.

Perfect Sight

A Worship Story based on John 9:38

The man bowed in front of Jesus and said, "I believe, Lord." (John 9:38).

Until then, he had known only darkness; now his sight was as clear as a newborn. Attached to his world of sound were warm, moving pillars. These living shapes revealed golden cascades of color, something the blind man had never seen until now.

Unnoticed since birth, he on that day, was the main attraction, the center of creation's controversy. People had never seen anything like it. Never! He was an attentive listener, with no fear of man. For what could be worse than total blindness? He learned patience from waiting on the rich to give him support as he pleaded for help, each day, sitting by the well. Now, the words directed towards him were challenging, and his endurance was thinning. "I have told you!" Rubbing his eyes, he said, "Didn't you hear me?"

Bad news travels fast, and for the second time that day, the healer came to the man's rescue. The questions were few and without religious politics. The man with perfect sight knew he was seeing the God that had done the miracle work. Without hesitation, free from opinion or trepidation of human threat, he lay down with great intimacy, worshiping Jesus, the son of man. Of course, the blind man had never seen true worship, but he instinctively, knew what it was.

Part Two: Stories of Worship

THOUGHT EXERCISE

When a person truly sees with his spiritual eyes the creator, Savior God, intimate worship is a natural response. However, we fail to see the real Jesus when blinded by religious service, thus, we fail to be true worshipers. It is a sure sign of spiritual blindness when we argue over a miracle or refuse to bow intimately before the invisible God.

The night I received the Lord, I was told that praying prayers, reading my Bible, and sharing with my friends was the most important thing. They said that my faith would be secured as I preach the message. Looking back, I see there was something missing; a step that no one told me about, a stride not written in the Four Spiritual Laws. It was many years later that I saw it, but it had nothing to do with my spiritual age, rather, my spiritual sight.

The man who was blind, after his healing, shared his experience with his peers building his faith. He spoke the word of God because he knew the scriptures, and all listened as he prophesied his future. Looking a second time, the man recognized the face of Jesus and heard the voice of truth. It was then his love overflowed for the Son of Man. His immediate response was to lay himself on the ground and worship at the feet of the healer, Jesus. The blind man's act of service, after seeing his Savior clearly, was to worship intimately.

The Story of Stephen
A Worship Story based on Acts 7

This was Stephen's reply: "Brothers and fathers, listen to me. Our glorious God appeared to our ancestor Abraham in Mesopotamia before he settled in Haran. God told him, 'Leave your native land and your relatives, and come into the land that I will show you.' So Abraham left the land of the Chaldeans and lived in Haran until his father died. Then God brought him here to the land where you now live . . . . "But our ancestors refused to listen to Moses. They rejected him and wanted to return to Egypt. They told Aaron, 'Make us some gods who can lead us, for we don't know what has become of this Moses, who brought us out of Egypt.' So they made an idol shaped like a calf, and they sacrificed to it and celebrated over this thing they had made. Then God turned away from them and abandoned them to serve the stars of heaven as their gods! In the book of the prophets it is written,

'Was it to me you were bringing sacrifices and offerings during those forty years in the wilderness, Israel?

No, you carried your pagan gods—the shrine of Molech, the star of your god Rephan, and the images you made to worship them. So I will send you into exile as far away as Babylon.' . . .

"David found favor with God and asked for the privilege of building a permanent Temple for the God of Jacob. But it was Solomon who actually built it. However, the Most High doesn't live in temples made by human hands . . . .. The Jewish leaders were infuriated by Stephen's accusation, and they shook their fists at him in rage. But Stephen, full of the Holy Spirit, gazed steadily into heaven and saw the glory of God, and he saw Jesus standing in the place of honor at God's right hand. And he told them, "Look, I see the heavens opened and the Son of Man standing in the place of honor at God's right hand!" . . . . As they stoned him, Stephen prayed, "Lord Jesus, receive my spirit." He fell to his knees, shouting, "Lord, don't charge them with this sin!" And with that, he died.

THE HISTORY OF WORSHIP

The history of the ages and the pages that held their story would be his security. Abraham, Isaac, Jacob, and the twelve patriarchs were his witnesses. The story of slavery and freedom, favor, and forgiveness—it was all there. The effects of famine and the misery that followed, along with Joseph's revealed identity, even his place of burial, spoke in his defense. The life of Moses and his bout with his enemy, leading him to the land of the Midian for forty years, would seal his case; nonetheless, "Are the accusations true?" they asked.

The answer was apparent. In his deliberation, the words of truth led him to what should have been his rescue. God had turned away from the people because of their false worship; they bowed before idols, worshiping shrines and heavenly bodies that could not breathe even though they had names. The history of the world was his story, with worship being the center of it all. Later that day, Stephen lay dead, and Saul, soon to be Paul, held the spoils. Worship has a history.

THOUGHT EXERCISE

The story continues. People who resist the most Holy Spirit chance losing sight of true worship. For it is the Holy Spirit that leads God's most beloved creation to the promise of faithful worship. The accusations and trumped-up charges brought against Stephen flowed

The Story of Stephen

out of a jealousy that was as old as the history books themselves. Stephen, telling the story of humankind, revealed the foundational problem found through all human history, which was misdirected worship. Standing before his accusers, the charges were simple. It was not the power to heal or the high level of wisdom that ended Stephen's life, it was the unfolding story of worship. The people were reminded of their past, which was now their present, and soon to be future. To refuse the Holy Spirit was to resist true worship, and they resisted. Stephen sees heaven and Jesus standing in front of him. In his final act on earth, he falls to his knees as his last words breathe mercy for lost souls. The story of intimate worship continues.

The Journey
A Worship Story based on Acts 18

"But since it is merely a question of words and names and your Jewish law, take care of it yourself." (Acts 18:15).

On his journey, Paul traveled through Athens, making his way to Corinth. While in Athens, the young traveler was struck by what he saw; he noted idols on nearly every corner, and in every meeting place. Troubled by the community's lack of understanding and the vanity of unknown worship, when coming to the city, he immediately went to the Jewish leaders to discuss the issue.

Showing devotion to anything other than the true God leads to idol worship. In Acts 18, standing before the court, the newly placed governor, Gallio, does not give Paul any time to plead his case. Instead, the high court turns to the Jewish community leaders and firmly ends their harassment of Paul, saying, "it is a simple problem, so fix it yourselves."

Taken out of the courtroom, Paul is severely beaten. All of this because of one word: "devotion." Paul, with theological accuracy, describes, using the words found in the Old Testament, true devotion. Devotion to many is more important than the act of worship—so important, they will kill over it. Like devotion, the discovery of intimate worship is in the words, the names, and the books.

THOUGHT EXERCISE

Do you think that a lifestyle of devotion is worship? If so, look up the word that Jesus uses in John 4:24 to describe true worship, and then compare it with the word that Paul uses in The Book of Acts, verse 18 for the word devotion. Then ask yourself, are you a worshiper?

If you are not sure, read the stories of those who worshiped in the Old and New Testament. You will see a design as clear as the heavens and stars that shine from the depths of space. Do you worship God's way, or are you living a life based on devotion only? As you read the books, beginning with Genesis, note every time you see the word "bowing"—then you will understand God's way. Paul understood the words, the names, and the books that describe true intimate worship; we can, too.

The Journey 2
A Worship Story based on Acts 19

About that time, there arose a great disturbance about the Way. The silversmith named Demetrius, who made silver shrines of Artemis, brought in a lot of business for the craftsman there. He called them together, along with the workers and related trades, and said, "You know, my friends, that we received a good income from this business. And you see and hear how this fellow Paul has convinced and led astray large numbers of people here in Ephesus, and in particular, the whole province of Asia. He says that gods made of human hands are no gods at all. There is danger not only that our trade will lose its good name, but also that the temple of the Greek goddess Artemis will be discredited, and the goddess herself, who is worshiped throughout the province of Asia and the world, will be robbed of her divine Majesty." (Acts 19:23–27).

The fearless traveler walked through all of Asia and the known world preaching the same message; know Jesus and worship him. This brought offense everywhere he went, for in each province, men and women religiously bowed before dead gods. And when they found out that there was a God who was alive, many chose to worship him in place of their idols. That is the message—Christ the Savior, the God who lives—worship him!

THOUGHT EXERCISE

For those of us who teach about worship, there is a problem ahead of us. The truth about true worship offends people. Why is that? True worship diminishes human ingenuity. True worship, the kind Jesus describes, cannot be fashioned by human hands. A person cannot build it; they can only allow it to happen. Secondly, good names lose their importance when people worship the way God intended. The acclaim individuals have achieved from their hard labor and sacrifice is forgotten when people discover the satisfaction of God worship. Thirdly, revenue produced by godly slogans and popular teachings lessens as worship increases.

Worship is not contingent on offerings for services provided. Worship is not a commodity, like a CD of music or a series of teachings streaming on video. It simply does not exist there. When true worship is uncovered, it breaks the pocketbooks of those who are in the business of constructing worship for a living. Lastly, when true worship finds its individual ground, and people bow with passion and intimacy, recognition as we know it, and the status as we find it in this world, melts away. Why is true worship so difficult to teach? Because people are human, and human beings want everything their own way. Intimate worship is a tough lesson.

The Simple Lesson
A Worship Story based on Rom 14

"As surely as I live," says the Lord, "every knee will bow, and every tongue will confess and give praise." (Rom 14:11).

"If a man is calling himself a worshiper, bowing the knee is the act that makes it so. If a person condemns or discredits another believer, how can they find comfort in thinking they are a worshiper?"

The teacher took a moment. Turning to the whiteboard, he wrote the most often misquoted scripture references found in the book of Romans, then added the correct words. Turning back to his students, he concluded.

"In The Book of Romans, the word *worship* is not found. Other words, however, have been mistranslated, such as working for hire, serving and devotion. It is here in Rom 14:11 you find the actual act of worship described in God's own words: 'every knee will bow.' Nothing is more essential than God's description of worship. Pay attention to it. The day is coming when millions of believers will worship Jesus for the first time. When at the return of Christ, every knee will bow. Knowing this, God still wants us to bow before him every day, worshiping with a bent knee before he returns."

The Simple Lesson

THOUGHT EXERCISE

Reading more than one Bible translation is a good idea, especially when trying to see the bigger picture. Consistent usage of words found in translations provides clarity and a well-rounded sense of what God is saying. In The Book of Romans, worship is described twice, and in chapter 14, it could not be any clearer. If we want to be what we say we are, we will have to bend our knee. I would suggest bending both knees—it is a little easier on the lower back, especially if you are older.

The Gathering
A Worship Story based on 1 Cor 14

But if all of you are prophesying, and unbelievers or people who do not understand these things come into your meeting, they will be convicted of sin and judged by what you say. As they listen, their secret thoughts will be exposed, and they will fall to their knees and worship God, declaring, "God is truly here among you." (1 Cor 14:24–25).

One by one, the men, women and children filled the room. With little space to move, they sat close together, touching one another's shoulders, squeezing in with their knees bent. Sitting on the floor, those who were late found a spot in the middle, in full view of everyone, the most uncomfortable place, having no wall to rest up against, and these meetings could be long. Despite the crowd, there always seemed to be space for one more. Whether a friend or an enemy, they would make room.

Those in leadership felt honored to see the people who were committed to attending the late-night meeting. During these meetings, religious issues were left for later discussion, while the homeless, widows and orphans were given priority. There was a lot to do outside in the streets.

In this meeting, calling out the surname of God was priority as Paul's word to Timothy rang true: "Enjoy the company of those who gather to call out God's name." This was one of those meetings.

The Gathering

At the top of Paul's list of instructions was one thing; when you hear God saying something to you, speak it out. Paul said it again, in Hebrews: "Don't refuse him who speaks, the prophetic brings answers!"

By now they had all learned what it meant to speak out; they could all do it, prophesying was a common word in their vocabulary. Everyone remembered the story of Paul and Barnabus in Antioch, the prophetic word that led them to their next destination, giving them clues to what lie ahead. It reminded them of the ancients like Jehoshaphat. In those meetings when the prophetic words came, revealing hidden secrets of the heart, these people did what Jehoshaphat had done—they bowed down and worshiped intimately in front of everyone—it was unmistakable—God was there, again. God's presence opens the door for intimate worship.

THOUGHT EXERCISE

God has a one-track mind. He is always thinking about us. First, he saves us. Then he gathers us. Then, with our consent, using our voices, he speaks through us, revealing the hidden secrets in a person's heart. Why would any of us have a problem with that kind of meeting, especially when it leads to the altar of worship?

Temples and Idols
A Worship Story based on 2 Cor 6

AND what mutual agreement does the temple of God have with idols? For we are the temple of the living God, just as God said, "I will live in them, and will walk among them, and I will be their God, and they will be my people."

"Therefore, come out from among unbelievers and separate yourselves from them, says the Lord. Don't touch their filthy things and I will welcome you."

"And I will be your father, and you will be my sons and daughters, says the Lord Almighty."

(2 Cor 6:16–18).

My paraphrase of 2 Cor 6:12-16 is as follows:

Paul continued to reason with the church in Corinth, saying, "Don't withhold your love for us! Do not draw back; you are like our own personal children, we need your hearts. We have suffered much for you and we want you to benefit from our sacrifice. Please, do not join in with unbelievers who say bad things about us. Stay in righteousness, not in union with those people who are not righteous. This is like walking in the dark. Who wants to live like that? What harmony will you find there? Nothing that connects you to Jesus! Becoming joined with someone who has never seen, nor believed in the light of Christ, and coupling yourself with an unbelieving person, it will not work out! Worshipers cannot connect themselves with those who are not worshipers of God.

Temples and Idols

If you believe in Jesus, you are a temple where worship should take place. God welcomes intimate worshipers.

THOUGHT EXERCISE

In 2 Cor 16, Paul draws a picture of the innermost room of the temple, a room designed for worship. Be reminded that the outer courts were not included in Paul's diagram. He was strictly referring to heathen holy rooms, as well as the Jewish Temple of Solomon and the holy of holies that once stood in Jerusalem. To idol worshipers, it was a room where idols were on display, and where access was restricted unless authorized. Found in this place were idols such as Diana, and other shrines that boasted of gold and silver.

Paul, after walking through the streets of Athens, made the connection between this restricted place and believers in Jesus, who now have the holy of holies, the innermost part of the temple of God, inside of them. Metaphorically, Paul was providing the Christians in the city of Corinthians a motif of the temple, which all the saints prior to that day, had attended. This temple of God was a highly spiritual dwelling for saints of all the ages who participated in worship. This observation was clear: "How could something so un-Godlike, be found in a place of that magnitude, the temple of such holiness?"

In the inner place of the temple, out of view from the human eye, bowing down and worshiping intimately was their act of service. Out of all the things that Paul points out in the second chapter of Corinthians, becoming this temple was the most crucial. If the temple in any way was polluted, the people's worship would mean nothing; even separating themselves from the world would have no impact if bowing before God was nonexistent. Touching something clean or unclean in a fallen temple would not provide any solution. With the temple destroyed, like the temple of Solomon, the relationship with the one true God and the power that he promises to supply is lost. The bottom line is, intimate temple worship cannot be compromised.

OUR SPIRITUAL MOTHER
A Worship Story based on Gal 4:26

BUT the other woman, Sarah, represents the heavenly Jerusalem. She is the free woman, and she is our mother. (Gal 4:26).

Since Abraham is our spiritual father, Sarah is our spiritual mother. Because of this, Sarah represents more than an earthly mother but a mother of a nation that would be in the future, free from the bondage of the law and free to worship God, God's way. She is not only a mother of nations, but as Paul says, she is the image of the heavenly Jerusalem, the altar hearth, the place of worship. Sarah, like Abraham, was a worshiper. Her life reflection displayed the heavenly city of God, as well as an intimate heavenly mother who understood true worship.

THOUGHT EXERCISE

Not much can be found in scripture about Sarah, other than that she was Abraham's stepsister, the second wife, extremely beautiful, and found favor with men, such as the pharaohs of Egypt. I would believe that she was patient, kind, gentle, yet serious and committed to the call of God. Sarah, like Abraham, knew God's voice and believed in his majestic power and purposes. This is what made her a good mother, as well as a true worshiper of God. In a land full of idols and polytheistic religions, Sarah remained faithful to Abraham and to God until her death. Paul reveals Sarah's reward when he gives honor to her name by saying she represented the heavenly Jerusalem, the altar hearth. Acknowledgment for being a true, heavenly minded, intimate worshiper of God is our spiritual mother's greatest reward. Intimate worship brings honor.

Too Much to Think About
A Worship Story based on Eph 3:14

"When I think of all of this, I fall to my knees . . . " (Eph 3:14).

As he wrote these words, the depth of God's universal plan overwhelmed his soul. The strategy was, to save people out of sin who had no idea they had sin; to draw millions of people closer to himself, even though they were unaware of the distance between them. The goal was to end a religious system of laws and commands, so God could bring more people into this prophetic family. The design included introducing peace to Gentiles who were too far away from God to find it, and peace to Jews who were too close to God to see it. Then, as if it were not enough, there was a temple erected inside of these new believers. One room, a holy, precisely prepared room for worship. If that was not enough, the gathering of people in one place under the direction of one spirit, using the gifts of the spirit for one purpose: to show the heavenly rulers and those in authority in the heavens that God was still in charge. It was, again, overwhelming. Finally, in Christ, all could come and stand before the creator God in his presence, ministering to him. All of this led Paul to a reverent moment on his knees, worshiping intimately.

THOUGHT EXERCISE

Paul, in The Book of Ephesians, received firsthand insight of God's universal plan for the church. The price Paul paid to deliver this information was one that none of us, if we were honest, would want to carry. Writing letters in prison is no fun task. Every painful word speaks of God's collective plan to send Jesus as a sacrifice for us, the drawing closer, closing the gap for the sake of the church. Personal peace, the prophetic family, and the building of the temple for the purpose of worship is the sum of this plan. Lastly, the Holy Spirit's gifts working in the church to prove that God is on the throne is the capstone completing the full strategy of God. Let us take a moment, thinking about all of this, until, like Paul, we bow our knee in sincere, intimate worship.

Every Knee (Not Just a Few)
A Worship Story based on Phil 2:10

"That at the name of Jesus every knee should bow, in Heaven and on Earth and under the Earth." (Phil 2:10).

Three things make up the world we live in: things in heaven, things on the earth and the things under the earth. Most of us notice the things on the earth. This is where we live. However, God sees more than just one dimension, and in his word, he describes other places that we are not aware of. Out of the three places mentioned in The Book of Philippians, the only one where Jesus's name is not fully accepted is here on earth. Many humans living on this planet have not heard the name, but the gap is quickly closing. When the time comes, and it is clearly on the horizon, the earth and all its inhabitants at that announcement of his name will bend low. At that time, whether knowing him or not, each person who is standing will no longer be standing. Those who are in bed sleeping will fall out of that place of comfortable rest into a kneeling position on the floor. The people who are sitting in their workplace will slide down like melting butter beneath their desk on bended knees. In a split second, bowing down before Jesus will be an actual occurrence on the earth. Worship will happen.

Every Knee (not just a few)

THOUGHT EXERCISE

No one is forgotten, not those in heavenly places or those sitting on earthly thrones, or those who have died and are now waiting below the earth in the place of rest, in anticipation of their release. All will bow! Those who do not know Jesus will find themselves bowing before him, and it will not be just a thought in their mind or a feeling in their heart. The word used in this verse is not the one Jesus used in John 4:24. This word describes bowing down, but without the affections of love built through personal timely relationship. Paul understands the magnitude of the act of worship. Having a heavenly perspective, he clearly understands what it means to bow down. Yet, this time in this verse, it is different. It is not a heavenly worship experience, but an earthly one filled with anxiety. All of us should bow, or at least bend one knee or the head, even, at the mention of his name.

Worshipers are worshipers because that is what they do; at least, that is what they say. Regardless of what human beings agree to, God gets the final word. We can bow out of fear, out of religious veneration, or with intimacy borne out of honor. I would choose that. You will see if you read the last part of this verse in Philippians that responding to his name in praise is also a rejoinder that happens during the moment of worship. The two are separate responses found at the same moment. Nonetheless, the verse does not say all will praise, but all will bow.

Syncretism
A Worship Story based on Col 2:18

"Don't let anyone condemn you by insisting on pious self-denial or the worship of angels, saying they have had visions about these things. Their sinful minds have made them proud." (Col 2:18).

"This world is a messy place! There are no boundaries or standards anymore, everyone just does whatever they want to, and absolutes do not exist."

Handing a five-dollar bill to the woman behind the window, he waited for his change.

"It is all a form of syncretism, a little here and a little there. Pretty soon no one knows what they believe or why, and no one seems to care, as long as the people are happy!" Turning to his wife, he said, "As long as everyone feels accepted, that is all that matters; that is what everyone is preaching, anyway."

Handing him a crinkled dollar bill and a few pieces of change, the teller waited as the man counted. "I'm sorry," he politely said, "this is not correct, you're a dollar short!"

As the woman looked again at the order, his impatience got the best of him. "Oh, just keep it, it doesn't matter anyway, it's just a dollar."

THOUGHT EXERCISE

Does it really matter? Col 2:18, the words "worship of angels" does not mean bowing before angels as a worshiper; it means religious ceremonies and disciplines that lead to pious self-denial, which in turn makes people feel less important. Shrines and statues of angels are the meeting place of confused man. Does anyone care? In Rev 22:8–9, worship is bowing before God like a dog who is waiting to kiss his master's hand; that is the definition of the word in Revelation. In verse nine, it states clearly, "Worship God!"

Angels, who have a direct link to God's throne and the ways of heaven, have reminded us of what worship is; the question is, do we care? A person said to me, "Where I go to church, we worship a lot of different ways. Everyone has their own expression, we just have to accept it." She then went on to describe praise.

It is much easier to leave it alone, but is that the right thing, even if it cost you something? The truth is, in the end it will cost you something, and that will be more than a dollar. Syncretism, *the amalgamation or attempted amalgamation of different religions, cultures, or schools of thought*, is widely accepted, but it does not produce intimate worship.

Lost Gods

A Worship Story based on 1 Thess 1:9

" . . . And how you turned away from idols to serve the true and living God." 1 Thess 1:9

After the devastating earthquake in Kathmandu Valley in Nepal leveled towns, roads, mountaintops, and the oldest temples on the planet, a middle-aged man stood before a crowd of people with tears in his eyes. News cameras filming, he cried out, "They are gone, and I don't know what I will do without them." The cinematographer behind the lens panned over the man's shoulder into the rubble scattered in the background. Piles of broken stones filled the streets with high mounds of dirt in nearly every portion of the city. Zooming in, the video revealed shattered ceramic faces mixed with carved images of foreign-looking objects, crushed into small pieces. "Our gods lived there in the temples," he cried, "but now they are gone, we have no gods."

THOUGHT EXERCISE

Paul had spent two or three weeks in Thessalonica, but that was enough time to convince the Gentile people to abandon lifeless idol worship in exchange for the living God, Jesus. Once Paul was gone, shortly after, the landslide of persecution began. Like the ground-shattering earthquake of Kathmandu, the Jewish community cascaded down to disrupt the lives of these new believers, but with no avail. The Gentiles of the small, insignificant city had put their hope in something much stronger than crafted statues that they themselves had once bowed before. Now the people of Thessalonica bowed, worshiping Jesus, the one raised from the dead, promising to rescue them from the days of coming judgment. The news quickly broadcast throughout Asia: these people bowed before Jesus, the living God. When the ground quakes, intimate worship remains.

The Lawless One
A Worship Story based on 2 Thess 2:4

"He will exalt himself and defy everything the people call God and every object of worship. He will even sit in the temple of God, claiming that he himself is God." (2 Thess 2:4).

"When the gloves come off and he is given a few short moments of personal glory, all that people have called God or made special for traditional purposes, will be wiped out and left meaningless. Then, when the man walks into the temple of Jerusalem, sitting down as if he owns the place, the real battle will begin."

The preacher wiped the sweat off his forehead. Taking a short drink of water, he leaned forward towards the congregation, his nose still dripping sweat from the heat coming from the spotlights overhead.

"When you see that happening, the end is near. Will you worship him? I hope not!"

Men and women sitting in the packed congregation shook their heads in unison. Waving fans beneath their chins and pulling the ties loose from their necks, they shuddered at the image. Even the children sat motionless, picturing the hideous man of lawlessness, like a monster from the deep ruling over the earth.

"God will unleash this lawless man at the proper time. He will no longer be restrained by God, but we, if we are still living, will have to choose, to bow down or not to bow down!"

The crowd of people gasped at the horror, as if they were watching a science-fiction thriller.

THE LAWLESS ONE

THOUGHT EXERCISE

What do you call god? Is it something universal, like air, or a shared sense of unity, steeped in spirituality? Is it a tree, or a cow, a fish, or the vast heavens overhead? Do you have physical objects that you possess that give you a sense of godliness and support a long tradition of religion? When the man of lawlessness walks into the temple in Jerusalem, pulls up a chair and says these words, "I am God," none of these vain ideas will remain intact. When you see this take place, you will have two choices: bow before a man dressed like a God, or bow before the invisible God, who rules the man. Which one will you choose? Intimate worship is a choice.

A Good Translation?
A Worship Story based on 1 Tim 2:8

"IN every place of worship, I want men to pray with holy hands lifted up to God, free from anger and controversy." (1 Tim 2:8).

"This is a perfect example of a poor translation."

Reaching up, he wrote the verse at the top of the whiteboard, leaving space for a long outline below.

"What translation do you have?"

He waited a few moments for the students to consider this question before he continued.

"If the word in this verse is worship, it is incorrectly placed."

The students quickly opened their Bibles to see what word was in 1 Tim 2:8. To their surprise, most of them had the incorrect translation.

"Paul was speaking to men everywhere. They prayed in the synagogue, the streets, their homes ... everywhere. These were not a place of worship, but places of work, socializing and family, community. Paul was speaking of everyday social gatherings. In these places, men were not worshiping; they prayed, and there is a vast difference. When Paul was speaking to Timothy, he described raising the hands high, *Epairo*, a literal expression of praise, not bowing low, as in the act of worshiping. This was a prayer prayed, not with folded hands and religiously bowed heads, but faces and eyes, coupled with lifted hands thrown out toward heaven. Not the posture of worship."

A Good Translation?

Moving to the front of his desk, he picked up a piece of paper and a pencil.

"Both of these items are used for the same purpose. However, they are different in their design. Both translate information, yet one is thin and easily torn, the other is stiff and more difficult to break. I would not write words with a piece of paper, nor would I write a message on a pencil. You see what I'm getting at? Words matter! If you were to translate this verse, what words would you use?

THOUGHT EXERCISE

Unlike praying everywhere, worshiping everywhere is far more difficult, and truthfully, it is not expected. Paul encourages us to pray, regardless of our surroundings, while worshiping takes space, time, and the ability to overcome self. Bowing down in worship takes no words, and the expression does not depend on the lifting of hands or the singing of songs. Like Moses, an individual can worship anywhere their heart is drawn, and the location does not matter. What matters is, do we understand the word? Do we call it by another name? What words do you use for worship? Are they words for praise? Probably. Intimate worship is a word of its own.

In Other Words
A Worship Story based on 2 Tim 1:13-14

WHAT you heard from me, keep as a pattern of sound teaching, with faith and love in Christ. Guard the good deposit that was entrusted to you—guard it with the help of the Holy Spirit that lives within us. (2 Tim 1:13–14).

Wear it, put it on like a shirt and pants, own it, being safe and sound, set in what is true, not mixing the world's ideas or corrupted beliefs with the words you have learned from me (Paul). Do not let anyone steal it from you, protect it the best you can, counting on the work of the Holy Spirit to help. Do not let it out of your sight. That is what Paul was saying to his best friend, Timothy.

THOUGHT EXERCISE

Everything that Paul writes in his letters revolves around knowing Christ. In these letters are subjects such as faith, love, living freely, being a church, ministering to one another, walking, and moving in the Holy Spirit, being bold and preaching, teaching, prophesying, and encouraging all those who believe to do the same. Paul's letters discussed daily issues, present and past theologies, scriptures, names of God-fearing men and women, and specific words. There is so much to learn from Paul that it takes a lifetime, and we still have more to discover. With each deposit of truth that comes in the form of words, we have the responsibility to protect it with the help of the Holy Spirit. What you know about worship, you need to keep safe. Bowing before the creator is a sound teaching that the rulers of this world would like to steal. Along with all the other truths that we have learned, bowing before Jesus is high on the list of universal bandits, and hackers whose goal is to hold worship hostage. Listen to Paul. Keep this deposit of truth under lock and key, not exchanging the act of worship for any socially moral idea, comfortable teaching, or weak theological concept created to please people. Intimate worship is worth guarding.

Living Proof
A Worship Story based on Titus 1:16

"Such people claim they know God, but they deny him by the way they live." (Titus 1:16).

There was a knock at the door, and the young man got up from the couch to answer. Opening the door, he was surprised to see a friend, one he had not seen in a long time.

"Hey, it's been a long time. Come on in."

After a few minutes reflecting on memories, the conversation ended as the young man's unexpected guest paused in a moment of awkward silence. Spotting a bookshelf above the television, the guest noticed the Bible sitting alone and covered with dust.

"It doesn't look like you have opened this very often."

Reaching up, taking the book, he blew the dust off the cover.

"I do, occasionally. I'm still a Christian." He said in his defense.

"There is more to being a Christian than just saying the words." He put the book back on the shelf.

Nervously, he answered, "I know that, but I'm not doing anything wrong."

Glancing across the small apartment, the guest saw signs of someone else. The purse sitting on the counter, her jacket hanging by the door. Without saying a word, the truth revealed itself.

"If you believe in Jesus, and call yourself a Christian, your life needs to show it. Claiming to know God means nothing; you need the evidence. The way you live is what you believe. You deny what you believe if you refuse to live it out."

THOUGHT EXERCISE

In John 4:24, Jesus paints a picture of worshipers who worship. The evidence is found in the action. People who bow before God with love, anticipating their master's response as they wait in his presence provides that proof. We might be good at praising, or prophesying in song, or even proficient at teaching and preaching, but those things, like I have said are not worship. If we do not live worship, in Jesus' terms, it is just a statement or assertion. Intimate worship needs proof.

The Home Church
A Worship Story based on Phlm 1:2

" . . . to the church that meets in your house." (Phlm 1:2).

"They left the community fellowship to meet in their home," he explained to those on the board of elders. "It was smaller, and it had a personal atmosphere, a real sense of family." He told them that there was no real order of service, which they had grown tired of. Now the purpose was the Holy Spirit, and they learned over time that God's agenda was exciting and unexpected. Trying not to sound overly proud, or hurtful, he clarified what took place in his house.

"Each person has the freedom to speak what they feel the Holy Spirit is saying, and the gifts flow easily. They have learned how to wait on each other, as well as on the Lord, which is also the purpose of the gathering. Encouraging words, songs and teachings, along with the prophetic ministry is common."

Looking around the room, he noticed the faces, some glaring, some with questionable looks, others with protected smiles.

" . . . And something even more amazing happens: people find room to bow down, right there on the living room floor. We have times of worship."

The Home Church

THOUGHT EXERCISE

Writing to the home church in the city of Corinth, Paul lays the blueprint for all future church meetings. The rules of engagement, if you want to call it that, were clearly stated and carefully delivered to the churches that existed throughout Asia; this included the home church of Philemon. In Paul's hope to reconcile the relationship between a master and his past slave, now a believer, Paul reminds those who worship in this home church of their reputation of generosity, which was found in their faith. Not only did these people spend time ministering to one another in the Holy Spirit's gifts with great generosity towards one another, they also experienced the grace and kindness produced by the Holy Spirit, which led them to worshiping with one another. As in 1 Cor 14, and the home church of Philemon, worship was the outcome of the Holy Spirit-led meeting. This leads me to believe that the church that met in that house understood the act of worship. Whether in a home or in an official church building, the meeting place of the saints should be a house of generous, faith-gifted worship. True intimate worship produces a reputation of generosity.

ONE LAST TIME
A Worship Story based on Heb 11:21

"It was by faith that Jacob, when he was old and dying, blessed each of Joseph's sons, and bowed in worship as he leaned on his staff." (Heb 11:21).

With the help of his two grandsons, placing one arm securely over their broad shoulders, he faintly steadied himself by holding his staff with the other arm. Riding on the heels of his twin brother, Jacob was born into this world, and now, 147 years later, his offspring carried the banners of the nation of Israel—the prophecy came to pass. Weakened from life's journey, his bones now brittle, and his eyes long since entirely dark, he stretched out his thin, fragile arm, blessing the two grandchildren. Touching their shoulders, he leaned over his staff, and it swayed beneath the weight of his frail body. Now too old to kneel on the ground, his staff became his altar, and for just a few moments, he bowed at his waist, worshiping Yahweh. It would be the last time Jacob intimately worshiped his God.

THOUGHT EXERCISE

What keeps people from worshiping God, God's way? It is not their age. It is their faith. Seeing God perform his word without humanity's help creates a faith that bows without hesitation. The faith worshiper is born when their dependence on God moves from hoping something, to faithfully believing in, through experience, God's ability to do all things. When a person who knows they are only as good as second best, and there is nothing in their power that will change that, seeing God as he creates in them a powerhouse; moving them from second to first place establishes in them a heart of worship that cannot be denied. In Heb 11, Paul does not tell the whole story of Jacob's life, but Jacob was not born a worshiper—he grew into it over time. The father of Israel gradually went from second place to first place, and he recognized it as the work of God. Unlike Jacob, many of us have sought out faith for modern-day faith purposes, and in doing so have failed to become faithful worshipers like Jacob.

Notice, out of all that Paul could have said about Jacob, worshiping was the last detail. Why was that? Perhaps, because faithfully worshiping the God of Abraham sustained him throughout a lifetime of long journeys and hard lessons, and like the staff of Jacob, worship was a point of stability. Intimately worshiping is something all of us should do, even when we are old and need a stick to rest upon.

Faithful Trust
A Worship Story based on Jas 2

"What good is it, dear brothers and sisters, if you say you have faith, but do not show it by your actions?" (Jas 2:14).

"The accomplishment of faith is the demonstration of trust. The evidence proven by one's confident actions anchors their belief in God's purposes. To say this simply, physical action confirms faith. In other terms, if you say you have it—prove it."

The preacher, after a sip from a bottle of water that had been sitting below the pulpit for the last forty-five minutes, called the ushers forward to take the offering. That morning, the offering was no greater than one a week before, and the week before that.

Closing the door to his office, he locked it, then doubled-checked to see if it was secure. He did it religiously, every time he left his office. Getting into his car, he paused before starting the engine. *They must not be getting it*, he thought to himself. Driving a few blocks, he called his wife on the phone.

"Honey, I don't think I have the faith for this anymore. Please pray for me. I don't trust these people; they just don't give enough."

Late that night, on his bed, his eyes wide open, his spirit felt restless. At that moment, an idea in the form of a voice spoke. "If you do not trust them, why should they trust you? Why would they trust me if you do not? Give and it will be given."

The next morning, the pastor's confidence was higher than it had been in months. He had found a sense of trust that had long been lost. No longer was he looking to the people of his small congregation to meet his needs; he honestly, with confidence, trusted God, and he was going to prove it the next Sunday morning. Sunday morning came, and before the service started, he took a handwritten check and put it in the offering plate. That morning's sermon was not the normal, religiously planned monthly tithe report—it was a sincere life story based on his trust in God. He never looked at the offering again, and for some unexplained reason, that month the small gathering paid all its bills and then some.

THOUGHT EXERCISE

It takes more than a deep checkbook to prove one's level of faith. Most sermons on faith that I have heard end up deliberating on the value and power money plays within the Christian experience, which, in some cases, places trust on an untrusted source. This is, to many, the Western Christian motif for faith.

Nevertheless, let us talk about the faith message of James, which simply states, "Prove it!" Do you confess trust in the life of Jesus? If so, show me—this is a simple abbreviated theology. Now let us interject the concept of faith to this spiritual premise of worship. Are you a worshiper? Prove it! What good is saying it if you do not do it?

To prove something, you must give a demonstration of it by the definition of the word and its meaningful action. If you trust in Jesus to save you and call that trust your faith, you must tell people, help people, provide for people, and teach people. If you say you are a worshiper of Jesus, bow down; this, too, is a simple abbreviated theology. Bowing is the only action that will demonstrate the word worship; nothing else will do it. Like faith, intimate worship needs proving—so prove it.

HIGH PRAISE

A Worship Story based on 1 Pet 2:9

" . . . But you are a chosen people, a Royal Priesthood (the full body of priests), a holy nation, a peculiar people, that you may declare the praises (thoughts, feelings, actions) of him who called you out of darkness into his marvelous (extraordinary, striking, surprising) light." (1 Pet 2:9).

Peter, in this letter written to all believers everywhere, was not describing a platform of worship, but a large worldwide group of people, so changed by God's mercy they declared in a loud voice, high in praise, the thoughts and feelings they had experienced. These human expressions, now displayed by human actions, Peter called a Royal Priesthood of Praise. When this continually expanding body of Christians saw the light for the first time, it was an extraordinary experience, striking them with power and surprise. The light was so great in them they exploded with praise. These people, miraculously chosen, understood they were a royal family, a strangely holy group who had something real, and they shouted it out!

At a time when Nero was preparing to burn the ghettos of Rome, making room for his own personal structures, people who huddled in their underprivileged shanties had little to be happy about. Who could offer praise within a city of oncoming devastation and destruction? Praise would arise from the ashes, not from Roman citizens, but born-again Christians. When praise wells up, it often leads to intimate worship, revealing a priesthood of royalty.

THOUGHT EXERCISE

What is the purpose of praise? What is the purpose of worship? Most Christians think they are the same. Strategically, and with great care, God uses specific words in his book to accomplish his works. This is what we find in 1 Pet 2:9. Peter in his letter to the Romans is highlighting the specifics of praise found in the lost form of the priesthood. He understood the history and accomplishments of praise. He knew well the act of worship, yet in this verse, there is no mention of worship. Worship is not a word for everything, even praise, as many of us believe. Nonetheless, we choose to make it that.

One must honestly ask the question, "If I feel like dancing with joy before God in praise, can I bow down at the same time?" According to the amalgamation of modern-day theology, we can. However, saying it does not make it so. Peter understood the purpose of praise as well as the depth of worship, and never did he confuse the two. During the reign of Nero, the royal family of believers were thrown to the lions, not because of their praise, but because they could not bow before both Jesus and Nero. It was one or the other.

Intimate worship is not peculiar praise, and for some people, worshiping intimately comes with a high price.

Adultery

A Worship Story based on 2 Pet 2:14

THEY have eyes full of adultery and are always looking for sin. They seduce unstable people and have hearts trained in greed. Children under a curse! (2 Pet 2:14).

"I'm so sorry. I do not know what got into me. It was like I couldn't think, and she was just there!"

The thought burned deep in her heart, and taking a breath was difficult. Closing her eyes, she stood silently processing his every word. Why? Where? She wanted all the answers, but then, she did not want to know. It was just too painful. Unable to look her in the face, he tried to say anything that would make things better.

"I will never do it again. I promise. I do not know why I was so taken by her. I do not love her, I love you. Please believe me!"

THOUGHT EXERCISE

What does adultery have to do with worship? In Biblical history, adultery was borne out of a time of idolatry, the worshiping of idols. As the people bowed before manmade monuments, the outcome was sexual immorality. Today, the people who struggle with reoccurring adultery are in fact struggling with impurity that comes from secret, unseen idols found in high places, such as the mind, the heart, the lack of self-control, and the selfishness that controls other people's lives. These are the idols of today, which,

Adultery

when left unchecked, lead to adultery. Therefore, the people of Israel were like a failed marriage when they bowed before anything other than Jehovah. The passing of time has not changed the result of sin. Today, idolatry will birth eyes of adultery, and sadly, sexual sin will replace intimate worship.

IF

A Worship Story based on 1 John 2:3

"... And we can be sure that we know him, if we keep his commandments." (1 John 2:3).

"Our assurance is hypothetical, based on a condition or supposition. That is, adhering to a prior prescribed guideline. You can only be sure, "IF". Following the recommended directions guarantees the benefits that come from the relationship of knowing Him. The question that needs to be answered: what did Jesus' share with us? What prescribed guidelines did Jesus' present to those who are believers?"

With a silent tap of his finger, the guest speaker lit up the tall screen behind him. Highlighted with bold colors, set on a darkened background, the scripture jumped out into the audience like a 3D movie. It read:

"You shall worship the Lord your God; him only shall you serve." –Jesus (Matthew 4:10)

"This is the first prescribed guideline. Before I continue, does anyone have any questions?" There was no response.

THOUGHT EXERCISE

What if all we had to do was bow down before him, seeking an intimate relationship with the one who loves our soul? What if nothing else mattered but becoming a worshiper—would it be enough?

If

Jesus said it is enough. The Son of Man knows that if a human being loves his creator to the depth of freely bowing on the ground without hesitation, that person will confidently rise to serve God in power. They will also discover that bowing down before Jesus is the prescribed priestly service. This is the service passed down for the sake of ministering to the Savior. If we can follow this proclamation, our confession will be surefooted, proven by the word "If." Intimate worship is the first "If."

Follow My Instructions
A Worship Story based on 2 John 1:5

"This is not a new commandment, but one we have had from the beginning." (2 John 1:5).

To succeed in a task, following the correct order of instructions can make the difference between accomplishment and failure. In his letter to an unknown Christian woman, John points out that the woman has read and knew the series of commandments.

Jesus replied: "'Love the Lord your God with all your heart and with all your soul and with all your mind.' This is the first and greatest commandment. And the second is like it: 'Love your neighbor as yourself.'" (Matt 22:37-39).

John reassures her that she will succeed if she follows the steps found in these commandments. The series goes like this. "Love God with all your heart, soul, mind and strength, this is the first. The second is similar. Love your neighbor like yourself." Giving your heart, soul, mind, and strength is sure ingredients for an intimate worship relationship. John speaks to the woman, mentioning one of the commandments, but she knew the others as well, and worshiping God, as Jesus points out in John 4:24, was one of them.

THOUGHT EXERCISE

Intimacy emanates when a person's life is given to God. This is the first step, not only in worship, but in service as well. When applying

Follow My Instructions

the intimate instructions that Jesus mentions, the order of things matter. For example, if you reverse this scripture, putting "Love your neighbor" first, loving them before you love God, as some people do, your devotional service will fail. You might appear to be doing well, as you follow the rules of ministry, but without all the working commandments in place, the balance of your activity will, over time, be unstable and will produce ill results. Therefore, worshiping God facedown with loving, heartfelt strength before one gathers themself to serve, is the most important commandment (See Gen 20, Deut 5). Intimate worship keeps things in order.

The Truth

A Worship Story based on 3 John 3:4

"I could have no greater joy than to hear that my children are following the truth."

(3 John 3:4).

"What truth is John referring to? There are many truths found in a Christ-centered relationship, and what John is saying in this text can be broken down into three categories."

Reaching over, the professor scrolled down and highlighted the words.

"*Respecting God, the execution of God's purposes offered through Christ, respecting the words of men while opposing the superstitions found in the Gentiles, and the inventions of the Jews, along with the corrupt opinions and concepts of false teachers found among Christians. To follow Jesus means in depth, you respect God first, worshiping only him. You acknowledge the works of Christ, but give up the misconceptions found in this world, and avoid following corrupt teachers of religion.* That is what John is saying when he writes, 'following the truth.'"

Resting against his desk, the professor made his last comment of the semester.

"True worship is first in truth. Jesus said in John 4, his father craves those who will worship in truth, always looking for true worshipers. The word *true* literally means the actual occurrence. Worshiping God's way, not according to this world's definition, or by the orders of religious teachers. This is what Jesus is saying in John 4. Worship is the first truth we believers should follow."

Closing his laptop, the professor thanked his students for attending his class, and like he did at the close of each semester, he wondered who out of this room full of students would apply what they had heard, which ones would become worshipers.

THOUGHT EXERCISE

There is a specific truth about the act of worship, and our Father's heart is glad when he sees it applied in our lives. To reach the altar of truthful worship, the filtering process must take place. A worshiper must sift through truths presented in the form of opinions based on historical religious superstitions, birthed out of theology tainted by false teaching. Therefore Jesus, in John 4 said to the woman at the well "that the time was coming" when people would worship, bowing down kissing their master's feet, thus meeting his Father's deep craving for worshipers. The woman, after hearing this fresh idea, knew that if she wanted to be a true worshiper, she would have to reevaluate the theology she had learned over her lifetime. This is an example of the process of true worship in action.

The truth of Jesus's words reveals itself when people are seen abandoning their old-fashioned and modern-day theories of worship. The truth continues each time someone falls at his feet, despite world opinion. This is the truth about worship; it comes alive when believers place themselves on the ground before the Savior King. Intimate worship is a foreseeable truth.

THE CONTENDER
A Worship Story based on Jude

³ DEAR friends, I had been eagerly planning to write to you about the salvation we all share. But now I find that I must write about something else, urging you to defend the faith that God has entrusted once for all time to his holy people. ⁴ I say this because some ungodly people have wormed their way into your churches, saying that God's marvelous grace allows us to live immoral lives. The condemnation of such people was recorded long ago, for they have denied our only Master and Lord, Jesus Christ. (Jude 3, 4).

Direct and to the point: that is Jude's letter to the church. Cain's crime at the altar, Israel's repeated idol worship, Sodom and Gomorrah and their hatred for God, false teachers infiltrating the church—do the problems ever end? Jude was not afraid to call things the way they were, nor did he hold back on what was to come to those who deliberately resisted God's clear plan. The truth about Jesus demanded a firm hand, and Jude carried it. The story told, true worship had clearly been compromised from the first sin at the altar of God, to the final return of God's judgment. Nonetheless, that was not the end. God is coming back to make things right again, and like Jude, true worshipers must contend for intimate worship.

THOUGHT EXERCISE

An editor said to me, "You sound angry when I read this."
My answer was, "Yes, I am!"
That was the truth. I am at times angry to the point of not wanting to pull any punches, telling it just how it is, like Jude. Why not get right to the point? People do not worship God; they just talk about it. Jude said, "I felt compelled to write and urge you to contend for the faith that was once for all entrusted to God's holy people." We have not contended for our faith that leads to true worship. What we have done is to accept something much less, giving the most holy thing over to our own desires and comforts. Intimate worship needs contending.

The Letter Carrier
A Worship Story based on Rev

I, John, am the one who heard and saw these things, and when I heard and saw them, I threw myself down to worship at the feet of the angel who was showing them to me. But he said to me, "Do not do this! I am a fellow servant with you and with your brothers, the prophets, and with those who obey the words of this book. Worship God!" (Rev 22:8–9).

Having seen the most amazing pictorial of the end of all ages, the man encounters, not the creator of the images, but the one sent to deliver the letter. Overwhelmed by the power of the mental scroll, John, forgetting for a moment who the master of the book really was, drops to the ground in honor and gratitude before the letter carrier. Out of all the words that had so colorfully described God's final closing act and sum of all sins, leading to the ultimate eulogy of mankind, a phrase that began in heaven centuries ago speaks out, "Worship God!"

John, whose heart is now overloaded with the universal blueprints of the final eternities, having seen more than any of God's servants in history, forgets the basic premise of life—bowing before the one who made it all happen. In the last book of what will become the bestseller of all time, this apocalyptic conclusion ends with an unexpected, embarrassing moment, exposing humankind's incessant struggle—intimate worship.

The Letter Carrier

THOUGHT EXERCISE

How embarrassed he must have been. Getting up from the dirt-lined cave, wiping the cold dust from his hands and knees. His spirit had to have been wrestling with such a great blunder. Like all angels, this one was a letter carrier, a servant like us, nothing more. The moment had been electric and over-the-top emotional, making it impossible to control one's reactions, but even that is no excuse to bow before anything other than King Jesus, Jehovah God, Lord of heaven's armies. How quickly the most spiritual can forget what is truly spiritual, and we need to be careful of such foolishness. Out of every apocalyptic word, the most powerful phrase is saved for last: Worship God!

It was intentional. God wanted to make a clear and final statement to all readers. Those who have obeyed the words written in this letter were to bow, worshiping God, not for the sake of servicing angels or institutions, religions, or created beings, alive or dead, not for a cause or a past spiritual high-water mark that someone remembers and wishes to return to. Everything that had been prior was a means to the end, the end being intimate worship.

Conclusion

Worship is older than the books that describe it. Yet, as old as it is, it remains new to me. It is sad to think that someone, a community or nation, could miss the most intimate moment with their creator replacing true worship with something contemporary. When I take my heart to the ground, worshiping, an ancient story comes alive: Gen 4:26 "when Seth grew up, he had a son and named him Enosh. At that time people first began to worship the Lord by name."

I bow before God because I know his name. He is not lifeless, cold or rigid, painted porcelain or carved wood. He manages all that is on the earth and all that is seen and unseen in the heavens. Eph 5:10 says, "Carefully determine what pleases the Lord." Worshipers bring pleasure to Lord.

To say it another way: to please God, worship him, his way.

Bibliography

Brant, Roxanne. *Ministering to the Lord*. O'Brian, FL: Mustard Seed, 1980.
Conner, Kevin J. *The Tabernacle of David*. Portland, OR: Conner, 1976.
Cornwall, Judson. *Let Us Worship*. South Plainfield, NJ: Bridge, 1983.
Elwell, Walter A. *Evangelical Dictionary of Theology*. 2nd ed. Grand Rapids, MI: Baker Academics, 1984
Reid, Alvin L., and Malcom McDow. *Firefall: How God Has Shaped History through Revivals*. 1997. Reprint, Enumclaw, WA: Pleasant Word, 2002.
Sasser, Sam, and Judson Cornwall. *The Priesthood of the Believer*. North Brunswick, NJ: Bridge-Logos, 1999.
Scott, Julius J. *The Jewish Backgrounds of the New Testament*. Grand Rapids, MI: Baker Academic, 1977.
Strong, James. *The New Strong's Expanded Exhaustive Concordance of the Bible*. Nashville, TN: Nelson, 2010.
Vine, W. E., et al. *Vine's Complete Expository Dictionary of Old and New Testament Words*. Nashville, TN: Nelson, 1984.

CPSIA information can be obtained
at www.ICGtesting.com
Printed in the USA
FSHW011219060122
87437FS

9 781725 268746